NO MORE BULL:
America, Please Phone Home

A LAYMAN'S VIEW OF "THE STATE OF THE UNION"

BY

CURTIS DAHLGREN

authorHOUSE®

AuthorHouse™
1663 Liberty Drive
Bloomington, IN 47403
www.authorhouse.com
Phone: 1 (800) 839-8640

Published by AuthorHouse 05/11/2015

ISBN: 978-1-4184-7539-0 (sc)
ISBN: 978-1-4184-7540-6 (hc)
ISBN: 978-1-4184-7541-3 (e)

Print information available on the last page.

Any people depicted in stock imagery provided by Thinkstock are models, and such images are being used for illustrative purposes only. Certain stock imagery © Thinkstock.

This book is printed on acid-free paper.

With a million thanks to:

My parents, Arthur Gabriel Dahlgren (1900-1988) and:
Signe Elizabeth Greenberg Dahlgren (1901-1978), and to:

My kindergarten through third grade teacher (died in 2004);
"Sorry it took me so long to finish the assignment, Mrs. Splittgerber."

To Alan Keyes, for his many endeavors that nurtured this project.

This book is dedicated, however, to you, the reader. Thank you.

Table of Contents

Is it kosher to be a realist?

September 9, 2003

Never mind, for the moment, why my opinions are so "opinionated," or whether I have my own 'skeletons.' "The world is full of fools," someone once said, "and he who would not see it should live alone and smash his mirror." The question really is, who's the biggest Pharisee, the biggest hypocrite?

The people who don't want to hear pessimistic warnings are the first ones who want to know if there's a traffic cop ahead (they may even have their own radar detector). When someone flashes his headlights at you, do you immediately accuse him of INTOLERANCE? Do you try to psychoanalyze the guy? No! So, who's the biggest hypocrite?

Paradoxically, the people who say that public servants "are ALL alike," and, "they're ALL crooks" are the same people who want politicians to micromanage our local affairs and personal lives more and more from far-off Washington DC.

The people who were first in line to promote the sexual "revolution" of the 60's and 70's are the same people who are now acting like fascists and "thought police" on selected issues.

The people who have always condemned our "Euro-centric" Western Civ now want America to be 'more like Europe' in many matters, including health insurance and morality.

The people who call the wolf ENDANGERED are the same people who call an unborn child UNWANTED.

The people who call "barbaric" the painless execution of a perpetrator of a cruel murder are the same people who think the dismemberment of an unborn baby is of the realm of "progressivism" and "enlightenment."

The people who are always crying "Separation of church and state" are the same people who try to impose the agenda of THEIR religion in the name of "Mother Nature."

The same people who favor billions of dollars spent on light rail, etc. (public transportation) are the same people who won't even let their kids ride home on the public school bus, circling the school with minivans.

The people who screamed about "book burners" are the same people who want to ban "Huckleberry Finn" and any book even slightly critical of Darwinism.

The people who send others to "sensitivity classes" are the same people who wouldn't hesitate to tell a young biology student, "When are you going to quit believing that crap your parents teach you?"

The very same people who took the Reds away from Marge Schott and sent John Rocker to psychiatric treatment — for their "insensitive speech" — are the people who just yawn when Ted Turner says Christianity is a religion for weak people or when Alec Baldwin says we should attack a congressman's family physically for the way he does his job. In that case, it was just a joke (maybe even a funny one).

The people who want "federal aid" for anti-Christian "art" are the same people who think a kid drawing a picture of Christ in a public school is guilty of "hatred" or "harassment."

The people who lampooned Ozzie and Harriet and the "Norman Rockwell America" are the same people who now want to "keep

2

it country" and save the "grandfather trees" (but "tear down all the dams").

The people who complain when a politician mentions God's name are the same people who lobby for "Deep Ecology" in the name of THEIR god, Mother Earth, "the Great Mother of the gods."

The people who used the "RIGHT TO PRIVACY" to institutionalize abortion are the same people who claim OSHA can inspect your home if you work out of your home.

The same people who teach that the human spirit and human nature are basically good are the same people who teach that Man is nothing but an animal and is free to behave like an animal if he so desires.

The people who used to ridicule a marriage license as nothing more than a "piece of paper" are the same ones who now hail it as the Holy Grail for gays!

The very same people who had a habit of saying, "Stay out of my bedroom" are now trying to impose external rules on private organizations such as the Boy Scouts and Christian schools and camps. Excuse me? I DON'T THINK SO!

Webster says that one of the definitions of the word *"bull"* is "a ludicrous or self-contradictory statement, **nonsense**"! These promulgators of psychobabble teach that religion is a form of mental illness, and yet these very same people hold to all kinds of ludicrous and self-contradicting **hogwash**.

The only thing these people are consistent about is that while they are selective as to which of the first 10 Amendments to the Constitution they believe in, they're also selective as to which of the Ten Commandments they observe. When living in LaLa land, words are subjective, so the word "unconstitutional" never matters unless their agenda can be promoted by its invocation. And any attempt to define "sin" equates with hatred. This false premise I reject utterly, and say, "Beware": such outlandish split personalities are not fit to hold offices of public power.

3

When they speak of *"tolerance,"* what they really mean to say is, "YOU must tolerate US — **OR ELSE!**" So, who are the biggest hypocrites, and why do we bow to their every wish? And, is it kosher to be a pessimist? Yes, unless you LIKE having your head in the sand.

America, no more bull; please phone home!

The 60-second seminar "...a few words now to Republicans"

September 15, 2003

Jeremiad, n, A tale of woe, grief or despair; a lament over wickedness or degeneracy, often used sarcastically. — Funk & Wagnalls, 1938

It is not a closely held secret, but when they are speaking among themselves, many Country Club Republicans consider cultural conservatives to be back-woodsy "one-issue voters." They have forgotten that their party was born and bred out of the fact that the Country Club Whigs considered the Rail Splitters to be "one-issue voters." One of the most famous but unread speeches of Abraham Lincoln is his speech in February 1860 in New York City at the Cooper Institute. This is the speech that "made" the Republican Party, but what is not well known is that it contains a little Jeremiad aimed at his fellow Republicans.

So often these days we are told that this or that issue is so "difficult" and so "complex," that — in the minds of the elite speakers — the rest of us will just have to agree with them and *forego all attempts to rectify the situation!*

We are also informed that in order to win, the G.O.P. must try to keep the great Center happy and even give the left some of the things it wants. Abraham Lincoln never heard the term "triangulation," but he had been there, seen that, in the Whig party.

According to the Encyclopædia Britannica (11th edition), the Whig party was "a coalition of opposition parties which influenced deeply and permanently the character, policy, and fortunes of the Whig Party . . . . Moreover as a means of strengthening the bond with their new allies, the Whigs learned to practice a tolerance towards the opinions and even the principles of their associates which is exceptional in the history of American political parties."

They had supported the Gag Rules of 1835-44 which had outlawed the mailing of "anti-slavery propaganda" and most politicians in those days hoped that the slavery issue would just "go away" or, in lieu of that, hoped for any distraction to take the people's attention off of it (the Mormon Rebellion and Indian uprisings served just that purpose). By reading between the lines, we can surmise the following facts about the Whigs:

They wanted to be *inclusive*; they wanted to *reach out*, to be *A BIG TENT ("can't we all just get along?")*. And so, on a Tuesday evening, February 27, 1860, the backwoodsman told a large crowd of New Yorkers that the U.S. Supreme Court was simply full of baloney on the Dred Scott decision, and he answered the question, "What would it take to SATISFY the pro-slavery parts of the country?"

"A few words now to Republicans . . . Let us determine, if we can, what will satisfy them. Will they be satisfied if the Territories be unconditionally surrendered to them? We know they will not. . . . The question recurs, what will satisfy them? Simply this: We must not only let them alone, but we must, somehow, convince them that we do let them alone. . . . What will convince them? This, and this only: cease to call slavery *wrong*, and join them in calling it *right*. And this must be done thoroughly — done in *acts* as well as in *words*.

"SILENCE WILL NOT BE TOLERATED — WE MUST PLACE OURSELVES AVOWEDLY WITH THEM."

The so-called "Party of Lincoln" could do worse than to dig out those words and read them again. Lincoln's words, like the Law buried under trash in the old temple in Jerusalem, have been long forgotten. This is not your father's Republican Party anymore! Like the Whigs, they are beginning to ignore Jefferson's advice: "In matters of style, swim with the current; in matters of principle, stand like a rock."

And it's time for BOTH parties to get back to their roots! Thomas Jefferson is supposedly the patron saint of the Democratic Party. In his second inaugural address, he said: "I shall need, too, the favor of that Being in whose hands we are, who led our fathers, as Israel of old, from their native land and planted them in a country flowing with all the necessaries and comforts of life; who has covered our infancy with His providence and our riper years with His wisdom and power, and to whose goodness I ask you to join in supplications with me that He will so enlighten the minds of your servants, guide their councils, and prosper their measures that whatsoever they do shall result in your good, and shall secure to you peace, friendship, and approbation of all nations."

Or, in the words of Lincoln, "Let us be diverted by none of these sophistical contrivances wherewith we are so industriously plied and belabored — contrivances such as groping for some middle ground between the right and the wrong, vain as the search for a man who should be neither a living man nor a dead man — such as a policy of 'don't care' on a question about which all true men do care — such as Union appeals beseeching true Union men to yield to Disunionists, reversing the divine rule, and calling, not the sinners, but the righteous to repentance. . . .

"LET US HAVE FAITH THAT RIGHT MAKES MIGHT, AND IN THAT FAITH LET US, TO THE END, DARE TO DO OUR DUTY AS WE UNDERSTAND IT."

Some of our "hipper" Republican contemporaries will say, "That was then and now is now. Whatever works!" WELL, as Reagan would say, and once said (in his farewell address to the United Nations):

"The deliberations of great leaders and great bodies are but overture . . . The truly majestic music, the music of freedom, of justice, and peace is the music made in forgetting self and seeking in silence the will of Him who made us."

Amen.

Whom the gods wish to con, they first make illiterate

September 21, 2003

There are some sentences that should never be completed:
    "America has been good to us, but . . . "
    "Thanks for the history lesson, but . . . "
    "Public education can be improved, but . . . "

Far be it from me to bash teachers, BUT- I am the education Establishment's worst nightmare. I attended a one-room country school and I learned how to read in six weeks' worth of kindergarten. I *overheard* more American history in first grade than today's teachers hear in 4 years of college! In fact, a poll recently revealed that most seniors in our 'top-notch' universities couldn't identify George Washington as the general of the Revolutionary army. There is a Santa Claus, but there is no "father of our country."

America's kids now know "Memorial Day" as "the day the pools open." They don't even know what the word "commemorates" means. I've run into three grads of the high school I attended who didn't know what the fourth of July commemorates. A fellow worker was once asked that question, and he said, "Fireworks!" When we gave him a clue, "England," he said, "Beatles!"

Even the majority of Brits today know very little about their Empire and can't even identify the people who are pictured on their money. But Elton John is a "knight"! Whom the gods wish to enslave, they first make illiterate, and this is all by *design:*

Prime Minister Thatcher said, "Be warned. A powerful, radical left-wing clerisy is bent on destroying what every past generation would have understood to be the central purpose of education — that is, allowing (in the words of Edmund Burke) *individuals* to 'avail themselves of the general bank and capital of nations, and of ages.'

"A society needs only one generation to abandon the task of learning and transmitting its culture, for that culture to become an alien, lifeless irrelevance . . . [and] the cultural revolutionaries will drown out what Lincoln called 'the mystic chords of memory' with jarring cacophony. . . . " *[National Review, 12/22/97]*

As her friend President Reagan had had the gall to tell the United Nations General Assembly in his farewell address:

"The deliberations of great leaders and great bodies are but overture . . . the truly majestic music, the music of freedom, of justice, and peace is the music made in forgetting self and seeking in silence the will of Him who made us." Today's schools are far more concerned with "self-esteem" than self-*control.*

The educational "Establishment" Mrs. Thatcher referred to no longer hides its true agenda. Did you ever wonder why "history" disappeared from the curricula and became lumped under the umbrella of "social science"? A few years ago at its national conference, the National Council for the Social Studies had as its slogan "TRANSFORMING CULTURES, Past Present and Future."

Which, being translated, means: "Rewriting the past so as to transform the present culture into a more politically correct future (my source for this information was from an actual badge worn at their national "conference"). **As George Orwell said, "Who controls the past controls the future; who controls the present controls the past [i.e., history]."**

This they have accomplished, incrementally of course. The very first priority was to say that the Founding Fathers were

Deists. Then after a decade or two of that, they talked about "a more *HONEST history*" in which the rest of the "myths" about the "founders" were tossed out. The natural next step was to simply stop talking about them in any way except negative terms (slave owners, angry white males, dead Europeans, etc.).

These "Establishment" educators want the masses to be just literate enough to read a ballot, but not so literate as to study issues on their own and make up their own minds (for that purpose, it's better to "study" TV and the movies than books). In Florida in 2000, they found out that some of their "alumni" couldn't even read a ballot, but in the long run they are achieving their *intended* consequences, their *designed* effects.

We have gone from one extreme to another. In the 1830s, the Philadelphia Public Library refused to keep any works of Thomas Jefferson because he was unable to "comprehend" the trinity, and therefore "pursued by relentless clerical hatred" (*"Jefferson" by Padover, abridged, p. 120*). Going from one ditch to the other, Jefferson is now good for just one thing, serving as High Priest for the freedom "from" religion crowd, even though he actually attended religious services in the Capitol Building and issued day-of-prayer proclamations as Governor of Virginia. He believed the states had more latitude in such matters than the Federal government.

In the bill for establishing religious freedom for Virginia, he said "[We] do enact that . . . all men shall be free to profess, and by argument to maintain, their opinions in matters of religion, and that the same in no wise diminish, enlarge, or affect their civil capacities." Tell that to a Federal judge today, and you'd better duck! We and our Commonwealth brethren have now come full circle.

On September 17, 2003 Canada's House of Commons passed a "hate-crimes" bill that essentially classifies the Bible as "hate-literature" (because of what it says about homosexuality). Quoting certain parts of it could win you up to five years in prison! This law is the long-planned result of decades of social engineering in the public schools. And these results are coming to a school near you.

Yes, Virginia, today's "Book Burners" are the National Council for the Social Studies, the faculties of our infamous "Schools of Education," and those who give them their moral support, including even — dare I say it? — your local school's "curriculum committee." Speaking of books, in just one generation we have gone from Treasure Island to Gilligan's Island to Fantasy Island to Temptation Island!

And you call this "evolution" Mr./Ms. Teacher? "What're you talkin' about, Willis?" You're trying to con me, right?

Abortion is killing us

September 28, 2003

"We are not sure that words always save, but we know, and are sure, that silence kills." —Doctors Without Borders

According to a poll published May 11, 1999 (USA Today), 21% of abortion clinic patients said they didn't get enough "privacy" in recovery rooms. "Those findings are reminders that women don't see abortion as just another medical procedure," said the chairman of the department of ob-gyn at Boston Medical Center. "No one who goes in to get their gallbladder removed worries about privacy."

In the May-June 1997 issue of Ms. magazine, Faye Wattleton said, "Who believes that abortion is something other than killing?" So why can't we all just get along and agree that abortion is not "just another medical procedure"?

In his speech to the House of Representatives on September 19, 1996 Henry Hyde of Illinois said, "I finally figured out why supporters of abortion on demand fight this infanticide ban [partial-birth abortion ban] tooth and claw, because for the first time since Roe v. Wade the focus is on the baby, not the mother, not the woman but the baby, and the harm that abortion inflicts on an unborn child . . .

"Dwight Eisenhower wrote about the loss of 1.2 million lives in World War II, and he said: 'The loss of lives that might have otherwise been creatively lived scars the mind of the civilized world'."

And it sears the soul when we justify the killing (Ms. Wattleton's word) of approximately that many unborn babies in the U.S. — EVERY YEAR — many of them four-fifths born! Do the math! "Run the numbers"! Get mad. Show the same passion over human life that you do over *tax cuts!* While we maybe "remember 9/11" most of us *try to forget* that more people die (babies) from abortion every day than died on September 11, 2001. That's just an "average"; actually half of the babies who die every week die on the seventh day of the week (which means *Sabbath* in several languages), i.e., some thirteen or fourteen thousand human lives every "Saturday"!

We react with euphemisms and catchwords: "Freedom to choose." "Reproductive Rights." "Women's health." "Planned Parenthood." In other words, "don't worry be happy" — just eat, drink and be merry — for tomorrow we ALL may die?

If we can justify this we can justify post-birth abortions (and we have); and if we can justify that we can justify "assisted suicide" (and we have); and if we can justify that we can justify involuntary euthanasia (the Netherlands formalized it, and we are working on it); and if we can justify that, as Raskolnikov said in Dostoyevsky's Crime and Punishment, "Man can get used to anything, the beast!"

The pro-abortion movement will someday smother under the weight of its own "success." After World War II, while America led the "sexual revolution" and most Western nations permissivized abortion-on-demand, West Germany's highest court said, "The historical situation in the Federal Republic with the bitter experiences of the Nazi period led to the establishment of a value system in which human life has absolute priority and according to which even apparently socially unworthy life must not be destroyed."

Unbelievable? You think this is some lie from an extremist "anti-abortion rag"? NAY. This is from the pages of The Milwaukee Sentinel (March 5, 1975): "Germans Remember 1930s, Reject Abortion" by Nick Thimmesch. He said, "The extermination of 10 to 12 million people did not happen through an overnight decision by Adolf Hitler . . . No, it was a group of Austrian and German physicians and jurists who came to believe, in the 1920s, that there were human lives devoid of value, and that it would be merciful to terminate those lives . . .

"In May of 1935, the Hamburg Eugenics Court declared that the interruption of pregnancy for eugenic reasons (or, 'racial emergency') was exempt from punishment, thereby legalizing eugenic abortion . . . There followed the 'mercy killings' of some 275,000 German 'undesirables' in state hospitals: mental patients, epileptics, encephalitics, amputees (including World War I veterans), deformed and retarded children. It was all clean, clinical and modern."

The pro-abortionists' claim that Hitler was "anti-abortion" is a canard; fact is, he didn't want his "Arians" to abort, or course (the pram was the first personnel carrier of the Third Reich), but *minorities* were a different story! Observers of German society in the 1920s and 1930s maintain the German people did not foresee the horrible death camps but were aware of the eugenics movement and "the new attitude toward the value of human life."

What a coincidence! Americans too just turn up the "bass" on our speakers so as not to hear the *silent screams*, and we lose ourselves in "Entertainment du jour," as if we were kings who deserve entertaining by a joker at the snap of a finger or the click of a clacker.

By the way, Poland outlawed abortion-on-demand since Communism fell there, and women are NOT DYING FROM COAT HANGER ABORTIONS. Germany, on the other hand, liberalized abortions after the fall of Communism. You say you're still "pro-choice"? THAT'S EASY FOR YOU TO SAY WHEN YOU'RE NOT THE ONE BEING DRAWN AND QUARTERED, OR SUCKED UP A VACUUM TUBE!

As Congressman Hyde said in 1996, "That we are even debating this issue, that we have to argue about the legality of an abortionist plunging a pair of scissors into the back of the tiny neck of a little child whose trunk, arms and legs have already been delivered, and then suctioning out his brains only confirms Dostoyevsky's harsh truth." Man is a beast and we can get used to ANYTHING. We can even JUSTIFY it! We can even call it "LIBERTY"! That's simply sick!

As Mordecai once told Esther, "If you hold your peace, don't think that you will escape in the king's house" (any more than the rest of us). That's good advice even for those who work in the White House. Given the rising popularity of involuntary euthanasia in the judiciary (Florida, for instance), if you speak up, the life you save may one day be YOUR OWN.

A 60-second seminar on *anger*

October 3, 2003

"Anger is better than laughter." — Ecclesiastes 7:3 (in 12th century English)

IF VINCE LOMBARDI were coaching in this day and age, he would probably be ordered to attend "anger management" classes. People today are taught to blend in rather than to stand out, and any expression of passion is considered not Psychologically Cool. Those people who don't "blend in" and who complain about attacks on their cultural roots are considered "not well-adjusted" and Lombardi wouldn't adjust well at all to the concept of "parity" or "outcome-based football" or "all competition is evil."

I used the term get *"mad"* in my last column without apology, even though a former President was lecturing California citizens that "whom the gods wish to destroy they first make *angry.*" I don't know who writes his stuff, but he echoes the sentiments of academia and the news media. The 1994 election results were called a temper tantrum by "angry white males." And no doubt this week's prayer rallies in Washington DC will be portrayed as more temper tantrums by those same pesky rednecks, never mind the gender.

WELL (as the Gipper might say) — that's weird, because I can remember the sixties when the SDS was rioting and university buildings were being blown up by fertilizer bombs, and the news

17

media never called them "angry white males" — they were called "idealists."

Maybe being "well-adjusted" in a world as wacky as this one is neither a logical nor a desirable goal. The other day, I was reading the King James version of Ecclesiates when I made a new discovery: The KJV says, "Sorrow is better than laughter" (Ec. 7:3), but the inspired Hebrew word for sorrow is the same one translated "anger" in verse 9 ("Be not hasty to be angry")!

This will raise eyebrows in the psychological community, and I wish I could say I've known this for years, but the hard fact is that the English words for "sorrow" and "anger" overlap because originally they meant the very same thing. Matter of fact, the Greek, Latin, French, and Old Norse words for "anger" and "anguish" also came from the same root words that literally mean "strangled" or "constricted" (our English "angina" comes from the same root words).

In other words, as the *"Dictionary of Word Origins"* by John Ayto says, the original notion of "anger" was **afflicted,** and "rage" didn't enter the picture until the 13th century. The bottom line is that those who "sigh and cry" over the secularization of society are afflicted by a sense of "indignation" that is justified. There is more "sorrow" than "anger" in the passion of a conservative, and more anger than sorrow in a liberal's passion.

In conclusion though, I want to preach a bit to the "choir": During this week's prayer rallies in Washington, you might take note of the fact that for practicing Jews and some Christian groups, Monday October 6th is the Day of Atonement. It is a day of solemn fasting that contains elements of Job's "anger, sorrow, and fasting" over his dead children.

The proverbial "Rachel weeping for her children" is a role model for all Americans today, and so — for many reasons — I hope that many non-Jews will also fast this year on the Day of Atonement. You can do it as a form of mourning our lost unborn babies, and as a form of prevailing upon the God of Israel for His mercy in spite of our attacks on the Ten Commandments and our Judeo-Christian Heritage.

I know a few "conservatives" flinch upon hearing the "Judeo" part of our Judeo-Christian heritage, but what can I say? That's exactly what our American heritage IS. The time has come to show how SERIOUS we are about "renewing America." It's time to get "mad"!

60-second seminar on "*turning back the clock*"

October 9, 2003

Two analogies that describe today's teenagers:

(A) Scientists have discovered a tiny creature that lives in the lips of a North Atlantic lobster; it is unique because its brain completely disappears at the onset of adolescence and doesn't reappear until adulthood.

(B) A farmer was driving a horse and wagon down the road with a colt trotting along trying to keep up with his mother. After a few miles, the farmer noticed that the colt had gone through a gate on the left side of the road and was now on the other side of a high fence with no gate in sight.

The first version shows middle school students being turned over to teachers and school officials at their most vulnerable time. And psychologists tell parents that, once kids reach age 13, any attempt by a parent to influence them won't have any affect one way or another (but drugs from the school nurse are a sure thing).

The second analogy shows the colt flexing newfound independence and going through a gate on the left. This often occurs at the onset of adolescence, but sometimes the brain doesn't disappear until age 18 or 19 during the freshman year of college. And, as Thomas Jefferson once noted, few in their after years have occasion to revise their college opinions.

The brain sometimes never reappears, but in the horse-and-wagon story, the farmer simply turned around and went back to the gate the colt had wandered through and recovered it. To him it was common sense. As a frequent visitor to the American West, I can visualize that scene right down to the worn-out cowboy boots nailed to the tops of a few fence posts.

Those of us who haven't forgotten our nation's cultural roots are accused of being "overly simplistic" and of trying to **"turn back the clock"**! Well, when daylight savings time ends, turning back the clock is "a good thing" and, if your colt has gone through a gate on the left, you just turn around and go back. No need for "parenting experts" to nag us about "how do you know the colt's way isn't just as good as your way?" Doing the right thing at the right time eliminates the need for "grief counselors" in the school later!

Don't look for a mass movement any time soon for "going back" to Leave it to Beaver families though. That kind of family doesn't provide any income for public employees in law enforcement or corrections, for courtroom stenographers or bailiffs, for lawyers or judges, for parole officers or psychologists, for remedial education tutors or psychiatrists.

Follow the money. I can remember when my county's "Human Services" department consisted of the sheriff and one volunteer who worked with a handful of "delinquents"; now it has its own multi-million dollar court house annex. And no one with "simplistic solutions" need apply for work there.

What's really hilarious is that, despite the obvious mushrooming of social problems under modern philosophies of education, parenting, and the media, today's crop of kids weaned on Darwinism believe the unspoken doctrine that they are **the most highly evolved generation in the history of the planet!**

A college student was once lecturing Ronald Reagan that the older generation couldn't possibly "understand" the younger because "we have TV, computers, space travel" etc. Reagan interrupted him and said, "Yes, and we **invented** those things!" My own father was born before the Wright brothers ever got off the ground, and he saw the Buffalo Bill Wild West Show and heard Teddy Roosevelt speak in person. He quit school after the eighth grade, but he could read and write better than most college freshmen today.

Not all "progress" is **PROGRESS** if you get the drift. More about "evolution" in my next column, but there's a joke going around the Internet that sums up where society stands at the moment. A lawyer had just picked up his new Lexus, and as he parked in front of his office to show it to his partners, he opened the door and a truck ripped it right off. With his voice-activated cell phone, he called 911, and an officer arrived within a couple of minutes to see the lawyer ranting and raving about his car and how "it will never be the same" and so on.

The cop says, "How can you lawyers be so materialistic? Why can't you notice the things that really matter?" The lawyer of course says: "How can you say such a thing at a time such as this?" And the cop says, "Don't you realize your left arm is missing? The truck took it right off when he hit your car."

The lawyer goes, **"OH MY ---- WHERE'S MY ROLEX?"** Follow the money.

[I have no idea if Rolex has one "L" or two; but I know that hell has two.]

Evolution: The Thalidomide of social silver bullets

October 20, 2003

When people say, "It's not **about** [such and such]," often that's the very thing it's ALL ABOUT. Believers in Darwinism often say that evolution isn't **about** religion, or that it is "neutral on God." Educator John Dewey, however, half a century after the publication of Darwin's theory, said that evolution had "introduced a mode of thinking that in the end was bound to transform the logic of knowledge, and hence the treatment of morals, politics, and religion." And I can picture him saying that with all the "neutrality" of Dan Rather announcing that the state of Tennessee had just gone for Al Gore in 2000.

One of the more honest Darwinists was Huxley, who made no secret of the fact that what evolution was **"about"** was freedom from traditional morals, for him and his friends. As for politics, Karl Marx wanted to dedicate *"Das Kapital"* to Darwin (his request was turned down), and as for religion, many theologians now insist that they are descended from some primate themselves.

An even bigger issue than the theory's scientific accuracy is its ramifications. Though touted by early advocates as a social cure-all for everything from poverty to guilty consciences, its actual ramifications have been specific and horrific. Darwin's *Origin* was published in 1859, and three years later, Russian writer Turgueniev described some of the consequences of the theory in *Fathers and Children*.

According to the Encyclopædia Britannica, 11th edition ("Nihilism"), the world's first hippies weren't those of the 1960s, but those in 1860s Russia, the forerunners of the Communist Revolution:

"Turgueniev had noticed a new and strikingly original type [of student] — young men and women in slovenly attire, who called in question and ridiculed the generally received convictions and respectable conventionalities of social life. . . . They reversed the traditional order of things even in trivial matters of external appearance, the males allowing the hair to grow long and the female adepts cutting it short . . . [They] had raised themselves above the level of so-called public opinion, despised Philistine respectability, and rather liked to scandalize people still under the influence of what they considered antiquated prejudices . . .

"Some of the Nihilists maintained that things were not yet ripe for a rising of the masses . . . that before attempting to overthrow the existing social organization some idea should be formed as to the order of things which should take its place [but] . . . in a brochure issued in 1874 one of the most influential leaders (Tkatchev) explained that the object of the revolutionary party should be, not the preparation of revolution in general, but the realization of it at the earliest possible moment, that it was a mistake to attach great importance to questions of future organization . . .

"**In accordance with the fashionable doctrine of evolution** [my emphasis], the reconstruction of society on the *tabula rosa* might be left, it was thought, to the spontaneous action of natural forces." So says the Britannica, and the "tsar" was assassinated in 1881 by those "hippies" (virtually 100 years to the month prior to the attempt on President Reagan's life by someone influenced by **our** "sixties" and 70s). Violence and backlash to it culminated in the 1917 revolution.

The World & I, August 1999, ("Darwin's *'Origin'* Transforms Culture") said this:

"The scientific search for truth takes place in a cultural context, and Darwin's theorizing was no exception. He unconsciously absorbed many social and political values peculiar to his time, place, and class; and these values indirectly colored his ideas . . . In their turn, social, political, and economic theorists appropriated features of Darwin's evolutionary argument for their own constructs, some of which were strikingly different from Darwin's values."

The eugenics movement and the Bolshevist Revolution are only two examples. The evils of all the wars of the Dark Ages were only dwarfed by the deaths resulting directly from the dogma of the various proponents of Darwinism in the 20th century. Ironically, I found a Wisconsin license plate made in 1917 that outlasted Russian Communism and its attempt to wipe out the Bible and religion and to engineer a secular "New Soviet Man."

Thomas Jefferson said, "I hold (without appeal to revelation) that when we take a view of the Universe, in its parts general or particular, it is impossible for the human mind not to perceive and feel a conviction of design, consummate skill, and indefinite power in **every atom of its compostition** . . . So irresistible are these evidences of an intelligent and powerful Agent that, of the infinite numbers of men who have existed thro' all time, they have believed, in the proportion of a million at least to [one], in the hypothesis of an eternal pre-existence of a creator, rather than in that of self-existent Universe" (letter to John Adams, 4/11/1823).

The term *Darwinizing* had been coined in the 1700s to refer to theorizing done by Charles Darwin's grandfather, so Jefferson had already "heard it all" and he still said that believers outnumbered non-believers a million to one. What's foreboding about today's secular movement is that John Dewey's public schools have used more patience and systematic methods than Russia's Bolshevists, and the scales are beginning to tilt in the direction of a million doubters for every true believer.

Is the evil genie out of the bottle for good? All the Founding Fathers could do is give the new Republic a shove in the right direction. The final fate of their high hopes is, without a doubt, **up to you and me — if you are up to the task, so help us God.**

Dedicated to Dutch: The reasons they hate Reagan

October 27, 2003

"These are farmers, the Common Clay of the Old West — you know, MORONS!"
— Mel Brooks in BLAZING SADDLES

In 1963, a couple dropped off their kids at church and went to play golf. Later they asked what the preacher had talked about. "Sin," was the reply. "He's against it."

In 2003, a latchkey kid went to church and was asked later what the preacher had talked about. "Hatred," was the reply. "And she's against it!"

WELL, if they're so *against* it, then why do the people on the Left Coast hate the Reagans? There are definable reasons. One reason is attitudinal: Reagan came from flyover country. By reading his farewell address to the United Nations in 1988, we can surmise some other reasons.

After covering foreign policy matters, President Reagan said his goodbyes by speaking like a grandfather to the third or fourth generation of his offspring. Can you picture this? It was a year before the Evil Empire crumbled and fell, and ol' Dutch spoke of the birth of the United States, how Franklin had called for prayers at the Constitutional Convention, and how Washington's

29

farewell address had spoken of the **Source** of liberty, how the case for inalienable rights and "the notion of conscience above compulsion" can only be made *in the context of "higher law"!* And he spoke of Family, "the first and most important unit of society."

"This morning, my thoughts go to her who gave me many things in life, but her most important gift was the knowledge of happiness and solace to be gained in prayer . . . I think then of her and others like her in that small town in Illinois, gentle people who possessed something that those who hold positions of power sometimes forget to prize. No one of them could ever have imagined the boy from the banks of the Rock River would come to this moment and have this opportunity.

"But had they been told it would happen, I think they would have been a bit disappointed if I'd not spoken here for what they knew so well: that when we grow weary of the world and its troubles, when our faith in humanity falters, it is then that we must seek comfort and refreshment of spirit in a *deeper source of wisdom, one greater than ourselves.*"

No wonder the Reagans are hated in LaLa Land. And if it sounds like I'm taking this personally, it's because *I AM!* I've crossed "paths" with him a few times in my life.

I once had a high position in Washington: it was Washington, Illinois and I was pruning a maple tree at the time (just a few miles from his alma mater, Eureka College).

That's another thing our elites can't stand about the Gipper; the closest he ever got to "ivy" was broadcasting Cubs games from a radio studio in Des Moines. But I've had it up to my vestigial gills with our Heritage being portrayed on TV as "extremism" and/or hypocrisy!

My own family lived for over 100 years in the valley of the Rock and its tributaries. My grandfather once farmed right on the Rock upstream not too many miles from Dixon. My grandfather died before I was born, but I know he would be very grateful that a President of the United States took time to remember the "neighborhood" in the UN General Assembly Hall in New York City!

May God have mercy on LaLa Land and anyone who would slander the Reagans, their family, OR their neighbors — the Common Clay of the Old West. **"FARMERS!"**

Morphing the world: Can you say "JADED," boys and girls?

November 4, 2003

"May we, like the Great Burden Bearer, tactfully enter into and share the needs of others . . . May we remember that kind words can never die." — A.E. Piper in God's Minute, Nov. 3

This is certainly not the topic I wanted to cover today, but I happened to read the 10/28/03 *USA Today*. A sidebar on page one caught my attention: STRIPPING GOES MAINSTREAM:

"Strip clubs aren't just dives frequented by men . . . Other than demand for dollar bills, **what does it mean?**"

Never mind the California fires story, I said to myself, **this** could be **BIG!** So there was the story about an Atlanta nightclub:

"STRIPPING'S NEW SIDE: DANCERS BUMP STEREOTYPES, GRIND INTO MAINSTREAM."

"As a dozen naked women undulate on 3 stages, Susan ------ fires up a cigar and leans back in one of the leather armchairs . . . The 48-year-old and a quartet of pals are in TGIF mode. 'Yea for the fact that women can walk into a strip bar without an escort,' [her friend exclaims]."

You can almost hear the writer, Kitty Bean Yancey, going **"Yea! Yea! Yea!"** And the phrase, "Just report the news; don't encourage it!" came to my mind. Immediately below that story was another one on L.A.'s Fashion Week, LaLa Land's answer to New York City's. A fashion analyst said:

"It's all very competitive. It isn't just about the clothes coming down the runway. It's this morphing of a world – it's sexy and visible, and a lot of people have decided, 'I want to get in'."

I'm sure the promoters of L.A. Fashion Week were jealous of all the ink the fires were getting in the L.A. Times, but there is something to this **"morphing of a world."** Something has happened to all of us. I've noticed that people of both genders can now walk past "sexy and visible" naked women at the checkout-counter without giving them a second glance. **And since when is this a good thing?**

Proverbs 31:10's pearl-of-great-price has become a pig-in-a-poke. NO WONDER this country has to spend millions on a little "blue pill"!

The word **"jaded"** doesn't refer to the stone by that name but to an older noun meaning (1) "an overworked, worn-out horse" or "a sorry nag"! The second-choice definition is "a low, worthless person, specifically a vicious woman; wench; hussy"! Hearts of stone are involved, though, and they're not diamonds or rubies.

According to the 1973 Mirriam-Webster Dictionary of Synonyms, the verb to "jade" means to **"tire, weary, fag, or tucker,"** and **analogous words include "satiated" and "emasculated"** [i.e., **"sick of" or "having a belly-full"**]!

Yes, we're almost completely **SEX-JADED** now and the only place the "mainstream" can take you is **down the river!**

Not to make this too personal, but my mother had 7 brothers and 5 sisters, and those 13 produced 55 or 56 first cousins on her side of the family alone! My dad's side managed to reproduce too (9 cousins, all males), so if I may speak for them, we would vociferously dispute the claim that *Playboy* magazine discovered and patented sex in 1953 or so.

A few words of warning to the "choir" now: For example, there was once a movie called "The Best Little Whorehouse in Texas" and one of my ministers said that that movie probably would have lost money if it weren't for all the phony "Christians" who saw it either in the theater or on TV or on video. And he's right!

Hollywood's charge that the liberation of Iraq is what suddenly made the Arabs hate us is as hilarious as the *Playboy* patent on sex. Islam doesn't hate us because we are "too Christian" or too "fundamentalist"; it hates us because we are becoming post-Christian "pagans" — the very thing Hollywood applauds!

Immediately after the liberation of Iraq, an Iraqi theater owner started showing American XXX movies. This may have won him some friends among his patrons and the western media, but it certainly makes the job of our military personnel awkward and deadly. For many reasons, but for this reason alone, America needs a spiritual awakening.

I used to work with a Mohammed who was born in the jungles of Indonesia, and he once said to me, "America is evil, isn't it?" He was married to a Jehovah's Witness, so he wasn't referring to religion. He was referring to our pop-culture. We have morphed into a Brave New Cowardly World. **It's time to get SERIOUS about boycotting LaLa Land. Amen?**

From LaLa Land to Ogallala: The paradoxes of optimism & pessimism

November 14, 2003

I tried to e-mail my last column to the *Los Angeles Times* and their computer sent it back as pornographic. By the way, in the column before that, I said that Mel Brooks says, "These are farmers, the Common Clay of the Old West — you know, **MORONS!**" Any idiot should have known that that was Gene Wilder's line (in *Blazing Saddles*). At least that's what my 60-something memory tells me now, and since I'm boycotting Blockbuster, let's just leave it at that. Matters of great importance bear repeating though, so I got that line out there one more time.

But I "ramble," as if reluctant to tackle this week's question: "Are you mostly an optimist or a pessimist? For the world in general, or just for yourself? For the short term, or for the long run?"

I often remember October of 1962 and the Cuban missile crisis. I was then in college at a brand new campus that had an all-freshmen student body. For some of those kids, being away from home for the first time and in a "crisis" really was like the "end of the world" and had some of them literally in tears.

But one of my fellow workers in the college cafeteria was cracking jokes. He said, "The optimists are studying Russian and the pessimists are studying Chinese." Well, I had chosen German as my foreign language, but with 18 credit hours per semester and working three part-time jobs starting at 90 cents an hour, I had more immediate problems to preoccupy me than international politics. I laughed at the joke, though, because I knew from biblical prophecy that Communism wasn't our only threat.

Our Founding Fathers were pessimists about human nature, but optimists about the future of their country *as long as human nature could be regulated by checks and balances and the people could "govern themselves" (in the context of the Higher Law alluded to by Pres. Reagan in his farewell to the United Nations).* Reagan and the Founders would all be pulling their hair out if they were around and fully conscious of what's going on now in the land of Columbia. They would think that our people must be having a collective nervous breakdown (not an original thought of mine, but true).

To keep this to a reasonable length, I will simply list a few issues that give me reason for pessimism:

1. The media slant: the fourth estate has become a fifth column. News and entertainment intertwined have become the Cruise Missiles of the Culture War, and those who try to react are accused of "divisiveness" (like a football player being flagged for "swinging back"). "It's only entertainment" they tell us, but as noted by Barry Farber, a German actress named Leni Riefenstahl (who died recently at 101) starred in "Triumph of the Will," a movie that made Hitler "a god with a not-so-small 'G'" (*NewsMax magazine*, Nov. 2003).

2. Federal judges make rulings that simply kiss off two-thirds of the American people (not to mention, the Constitution). Replacement judicial appointees are held hostage. State justices are dismissed for making waves in the ocean of political correctness. And if anyone goes, "What's going on here?," the news media spin them as pro-gun fanatics. Huh? [see #1] The federal courts have become the Stealth bombers of the Culture War, and sometimes Supreme Court decisions are used later to do the opposite of the "original intent." In Brown v. Board of Education, the young student wanted to go to one particular school because it was *across the street (not because it was a white school)*, but that decision was used later to justify cross-town busing!

3. General overconfidence: during the nineties, President Clinton announced that we had "beaten the business

cycle." We have won the Cold War, and the H-bomb of Dr. Edward Teller (who also died recently) is credited with "breaking the cycle of wars every 20 years between nation-states." Optimists would say that since the world outlived the "Dr. Strangelove," who, some people thought, would destroy it, that's a good sign. Pessimists such as I would say that the exit of a great "Restrainer" such as Dr. Teller could be an event of biblical magnitude. In case you hadn't noticed, wars continue between "pseudo-nations" and our ultimate undoing could come from a non sequitur called Palestine.

4. The economy, stupid: coming events cast their shadows before, and the weakening of the dollar is portended by our trade deficits, personal and national debt, and even the low interest rates. Mainstream economists say trade deficits are harmless, because foreign countries invest their excess money in U.S. dollar bills. Question: what happens when the Euro becomes more desired than the dollar? Just asking.

5. Basic problems with agriculture: There were two warm winters starting in 1930 and 1931, and five years of Dust Bowl drought followed (that was NOT Global Warming caused by the Model Ts on the freeways). We've already had the 2 warm winters. Thousands of people were killed by heat in Europe last summer, and the California fires could be just the beginning. Keep one eye on the sky and the other one on the decline of water levels in the Great Lakes and the Ogallala aquifer (you know, those little green crop circles in flyover country — they are fed by wells that are dropping much faster than normal replenishment rates). I could cite the stats, but you don't even want to know about it.

Bottom line is, the spike in religious awareness after 9/11 has gone below flat-line. Kids don't want to be like Mike; they don't even want to be like Ken and Barbie; they want to be like Monica and Bubba. Hollywood **still** wants to demonize Ron and Nancy on Showtime, but who is calling whom dysfunctional?

About two years ago, a special publication called "Hollywood Tragedies . . . the price of fame" contained 32 pages of stories on dysfunctional families and premature deaths in LaLa Land

(*National Enquirer*). Michael Douglas' son had been arrested 8 times, yet Tinseltown wants to make a big deal of Patti Reagan's childhood tantrums? What's that all about, as they say out there?

Wake up, folks! We're not in Kansas anymore, Toto. And this certainly ain't **Camelot either!** Time to pray for some brains and some heart and some courage.

THINK-giving Day and what really made America great

November 20, 2003

"From the heart come evil thanks."
— Old English translation of Matthew 15:19

Nothing throws new light on a subject like discovering the ancient origins of a word. Here's "everything you wanted to know about *thanksgiving* but were too stuffed to ask," plus some points on what made America the greatest nation on earth.

The primitive roots of the word *"thank"* go back to the prehistoric Germanic *thengk* (as in today's *denken*, or, THINK). "Gratitude" wasn't involved in the word *thank* until the 14th century, evolving from "thought" to "favourable thought" to "gratitude" (according to John Ayto in the *Dictionary of Word Origins*).

Thus, "THOUGHTS" and "THANKS" came to overlap! Gratitude should follow thought as logically as the sunrise follows the sunset **so,** Thanksgiving Day isn't an emotional "superstition" or simplistic "sentimentality," but the epitome of reason and rationality, a joint effort of the heart and the MIND!

When Christ broke bread and gave thanks, the Greek word for "thanks" alludes to an open hand, as one plucking an instrument in celebration or praise. I will assume that you "celebrate" the

41

holiday, even though some people are so offended by their own presence in the New World that they don't celebrate Thanksgiving. Other people may eat turkey but don't really give their Creator the credit for America's blessings.

Many teachers credit modern education while bureaucrats credit social programs and regulation. "Labor" credits the unions and MBAs credit business. People may give the glory to FDR or JFK or 401Ks. No one asks the farmer, but as Lincoln said, we quickly became a great power due to the fact that God had given us "the richest soil in the most salubrious climes of the earth." Put me down as agreeing with Lincoln.

Our physical blessings were a great, unearned gift. However, individual leaps of great FAITH were required to access the grace God shed on thee, America. The Pilgrims did not have a cruise insurance policy underwritten by some international corporation. Their positive relationship with the Indians wasn't part of a "package deal" at a casino!

Our Founding Fathers didn't have social "Security," but they burned their bridges to Europe. The mountain men didn't have a computer program to show them the best routes, but they "paved" the way. The Pioneers made it to Utah and points west without a Department of Transportation!

The 49ers didn't have any "affirmative action" but they "diversified" California and helped build Fort Knox (if the country had had as many environmental "protection" lawyers as we have now, the railroads wouldn't have had any steel for their trains or tracks, let alone a golden spike to drive)!

Teen-aged "school marms" taught generation after generation how to read — without teaching certificates — and they even taught English and grammar, which some of our schools now don't even **attempt. And between blasting stumps and building buildings, the farmers farmed, the "the MORONS"!**

All of the above were great leaps of faith with no guarantees. My grandfather farmed 500 acres with horses, plus he peddled the milk door-to-door in town. One of his favorite sayings was, "Thank

God for the rich people, because the poor people don't have any money." By that he meant that after the rich paid their bills, he could break even at the end of the week despite the "free" milk given to poor people who couldn't pay the bill.

When Ronald Reagan's family lived in South Chicago, his brother was sent once a week to the butcher shop with a dime for a soup bone and instructions to ask for a free liver "for the cat" (*they didn't have a cat*). The throw away liver was their Sunday dinner, and the bone was for the soup pot that was kept on the stove all week. But Ronald Reagan often said, "I suppose we were poor, but we never knew we were poor." — *Ronald Reagan, His Story in Pictures* by Stanley P. Friedman

Many people before and since have expressed the same sentiment in those very same words, no plagiarism intended. That's the very essence of **thanksgiving, and did you ever notice, it's easier to be thankful for a soup bone than for great abundance?**

Only if you've been there, done that, I suppose. Obesity is now a big problem with our lower classes (who are sometimes our biggest complainers). And my point is: even the weekly soup bone had to be produced by some "dumb farmer" like my grampa, or my dad (who never owned his own land until he was in his fifth decade).

I did my share of driving horses too, and started driving tractor even earlier at the age of 5. I know a farm girl who started driving tractor for her dad at the age of four (girls are more mature than boys at early ages)! Even today, don't assume that your Thanksgiving dinner was produced by machines and robots without human effort, or human sacrifices. I know farmers who lost limbs and various body parts, and even children, in the process of producing your food.

So that's a couple of points, and you want to know another thing that irritates me? City people complain if it should rain on the weekend. Poets and songwriters say things such as "Raindrops Keep Falling on my Head," "Don't rain on my parade," etc. City people just **love** it if it doesn't rain for a couple of months; disc jockeys go on and on about the "gorgeous" and "sensational" golfing weather. One more Dust Bowl and these city folks are going to run plum out of superlatives.

"Out of the heart of man proceed evil *thoughts* and evil *thanks.*" But you have a nice weekend, hear?

P.S. The last word in Thanksgiving is *"giving"* — *as in "the sacrifices of thanksgiving."* What are you planning to sacrifice for Thanksgiving? Maybe someone out there needs a soup bone.

Truth or CONSEQUENCES: on chopping down a redwood tree

December 3, 2003

We live in the age of "safe sin" in which anything and everything is tolerated except "intolerance" and anger. I once had the pleasure of attending an "anger management" class. The instructor was an openly proud graduate of the University of Chicago (where a men's room used to be a men's room and the women were glad of it, but now they're not so sure anymore). You know — "shades of gray"!

Anyway, one day this guy said (with great sarcasm): "Some people believe that America is going to hell in a hay basket."

"HANDBASKET," I yelled! He wasn't impressed. I had to come up with a better way to tweak him, so one day during a lull in class, I casually said, "I cut down a redwood tree one time."

He almost went postal on me. "It was a dead one," I added, but his glare turned to daggers. I didn't want to have to do CPR on him or something, so I didn't bother finishing the story (how it was a "baby" 100-footer and deader than a door-nail, how the owner was trying to create a fire barrier around his house). You might say it was nothing more than a redwood miscarriage or abortion)!

Steam was about to come out of his red ears, so I dropped the subject, but the whole thing was a valuable learning experience.

One of his philosophies was that after an offspring reaches the age of 13, no amount of influence by a parent has any effect whatsoever one way or another. Now that's leftist bull, because if you touch one of THEIR hot buttons, "moral relativism" and "understanding" go out the window and they become flaming rednecks!

"How DARE you?" "That's UNACCEPTABLE!" "Almost INAPPROPRIATE even!" "How perverted!!"

Which reminds me: on the day after Thanksgiving, ABC's 20-20 program had an interview with the founder of *Playboy* in connection with its 50th anniversary. The interviewee was asked, "Do you think you've 'won'?" [i.e., the culture war, or in other words, is God finally dead?]

"Yes," he responded. I hate to have to tell him, but the only thing he's 'won' is the booby prize.

I cannot tell a lie; I did cut down a redwood tree, but this column isn't about Sequoias. The word for the day is consequences, which literally means "with sequences." Sequences is from a family of English words that go back to the Latin words *sequi* and *seqela*, which in turn mean to follow and that which follows, or, "sequel"!

One would think that LaLa Land would understand the word SEQUEL, wouldn't one? The word is related to "subsequent" or "result," as in "ye shall reap what ye SOW"! Even the word *lawsuit* goes back to the roots of "consequences"!

By the way: on the day after the day after Thanksgiving, the Democrat Party response to the President's weekly radio message contained an uncharacteristic reference to our Founding Fathers. For 50 years, the left has obviously shown that they can't stand a single word the Founders ever wrote, and as the founder of *Playboy* indicates, they've "WON"! Why the sudden allusion to the Founding Fathers when they still don't agree with the Founders?

For example, Benjamin Franklin once said that sin is forbidden because it is harmful, not harmful because it is 'verboten' (I think you get the drift).

My next column will have more words of the Founders on the subject of consequences. In conclusion, I only used the word redwood in the title today like a bullfighter uses a red cape: to attract as many left-leaning readers to this column as possible. It's just a coincidence that "Sequoia" sounds something like sequi; Sequoia comes from a Cherokee word that's evidently unrelated.

Tinseltown and "Friends" are more grieved by the death of a tree or a whale or a wolf than the death of their own offspring (fetus is the Latin word for offspring)! And they think they've WON something? Hee Haw!

The justices' new robes: gold-threaded or cold-blooded?

December 11, 2003

Unborn baby: "*Mommy, Mommy — what does abortion have to do with the 'Right to Privacy'?*"

Mommy: "*Shut up and leave me and your father ALONE!*"

Baby (a few years later): "*Mommy, Mommy — now that I survived the abortion, can you tell me what does campaign finance have to do with corruption of government?*"

Mommy: "*Shut up and leave me and your stepfather ALONE! And stop calling me Mommy!*"

"*Yes, your honor.*"

Well, those conversations may or may not be imaginary, but really, December 11, 2003, will go down as a day of Infamy in the history of our Republic. Five-to-four, the Supreme Court sold itself out. They confused impudence with jurisprudence. Which part of "Congress shall make no law restricting free speech" do they not understand? Even the ACLU is confused.

Not to rain on their charade, but not since the Gag Rules of 1835-1844 have all three branches of our Federal government gone on record as gung-ho against Freedom of Speech. Whatever happened to the "chilling effect" our leftist friends were decrying when CBS scuttled "The Reagans" mini-series (without any government involvement, I might add)?

The reality is, CBS and ABC, etc., will be able to use "poetic license" and "literary creativity" in the news within 60 days of a general election, and the groups they attack, such as right-to-life groups, will not be ALLOWED by law to respond! The SCOTUS has ruled that virtual child porn and cable pornography is speech "protected by the Constitution" but a group that uses soft money to mention an incumbent's name in a TV ad within 60 days of the election will be classified as a "criminal" group. What more could be "chilling"?

Even eternally optimistic conservative commentators are shocked. I'm not. Neither eternally optimistic nor shocked! History doesn't repeat itself *precisely*, but nothing that does happen should ever surprise us anymore! Not when perhaps 95% of our population didn't even notice this happen, let alone understand the ramifications. Now that the NRL and the NRA have, essentially, been silenced in elections, it's only a matter of time before Big Brother tries to silence or regulate the very media that supported this (stuff)!

Here's an excerpt from a daily reading I do:

> Years ago, an ambassador from another country came to Sparta, a city which, unlike most others in Greece at that time, had no walls. "The city is very fine," he said, "but where are your walls?"
>
> He was taken outside the city to see the Spartan army lined up all around it . . . "These are the walls of Sparta," said the guide.
>
> In a truer sense than that . . . the men and women and children of a nation are its defense, "the living stones" in its wall. —*Today With God* (December 11th)

This, the *true* wall of "separation" protecting the churches from the government, is being broken down chink by chink, exposing us to greater dangers than either Terrorism or the measures created to combat it. Our Founding Fathers cited Life, Liberty, and the Pursuit of Happiness as a sort of tri-pod of the Union, but with Life and Free Speech no longer sacred, how can the Union stand on one leg? "Happiness" so based and so pursued will soon evaporate from the earth, if this is "the last best hope for man"!

On the Jefferson Memorial are chiseled these words: "The God who gave us life, gave us liberty at the same time." And on the facade of the Federal Court House in Sioux City, Iowa, the engraved words say: "Mercy and justice are met together" (a quote from Psalm 85:10). How vain can some people be to think that they can "unchisel" all these words, or erase the Ten Commandments (which probably still exist somewhere on earth, wherever the ark of the covenant is hidden)?

Jefferson would be dumb-founded by today's anti-Jeffersonian "Judges"! His personally written epitaph says: "Author of the Declaration of Independence and the Statute of Virginia for Religious Freedom — and Father of the University of Virginia." I wonder if William Jefferson Blythe Clinton would be able to cite his 3 most interesting achievements without mentioning President of the United States, but anyway:

In the said statute for Religious Freedom in Virginia, it says: "We the General Assembly of Virginia do enact that no man shall be compelled to frequent or support any religious worship, place, or ministry whatsoever, nor shall be enforced, restrained, molested, or burthened in his body or goods, OR SHALL OTHERWISE SUFFER, ON ACCOUNT OF HIS RELIGIOUS OPINIONS OR BELIEF; BUT THAT ALL MEN SHALL BE FREE TO PROFESS, AND BY ARGUMENT TO MAINTAIN, their opinions in matters of religion, and [are you ready for this?] THAT THE SAME IN NO WISE DIMINISH, ENLARGE, OR AFFECT THEIR CIVIL CAPACITIES."

And yet, two judges in the southern circus say that JUDGE MOORE MUST RECANT OR FOREVER HOLD HIS PEACE [BECAUSE: "WE MUST NOT 'acknowledge' THE NAME OF THE LORD." —Amos 6:10] By the standards of the Attorney General of Alabama, most of our early Presidents were "disqualified" from serving in a "civil capacity" because they mentioned God and actually prayed at the podium!

In his first inaugural, Jefferson expressed "support of the State governments in all their rights as the most competent administra[tors] for our domestic concerns and the surest bulwarks against anti republican tendencies" and he closed the address with these words:

> And may that Infinite Power which rules the destinies of the universe lead our councils to what is best, and give them favorable issue for your peace and prosperity.
> —March 4, 1801

Dittoes, March 4, 1805: "I shall need too, the favor of that Being in whose hands we are, who led our fathers, *as Israel of old*, from their native land and planted them in a country flowing with all the necessaries and comforts of life; who has covered our infancy with His providence and our riper years with His wisdom and power, and to whose goodness I ASK YOU TO JOIN IN SUPPLICATIONS WITH ME THAT HE WILL SO ENLIGHTEN THE MINDS OF YOUR SERVANTS, GUIDE THEIR COUNCILS, AND PROSPER THEIR MEASURES THAT WHATSOEVER THEY DO SHALL RESULT IN YOUR GOOD, AND SHALL SECURE TO YOU THE PEACE, FRIENDSHIP, AND APPROBATION OF ALL NATIONS." —2nd inaugural address

As hinted at by my last column, there are such things as CONSEQUENCES. In *"Notes on Virginia,"* Jefferson asked two "dumb questions": "Can the liberties of a nation be thought secure when we have removed their only firm basis, a conviction in the minds of the people that these liberties are . . . the gift of God? THAT THEY ARE NOT TO BE VIOLATED BUT WITH HIS WRATH?"

Thus we have come full circle, linking McCain-Feingold to all the other "issues" being glamorized by Federal courts and the increasingly secular Supreme Court, plus the Massachusetts Supreme court. We have met the enemy, *within!*

Column of the year: Grading 2003 A.D., on the curve

December 26, 2003

"Despotism may govern without faith, but liberty cannot."
— Alexis de Tocqueville

IN "THE END OF HISTORY," an Op Ed, Lynn Cheney said, "Imagine an outline for the teaching of history in which George Washington makes only a fleeting appearance and is never described as our first President . . . that not a single one of the 31 standards mentions the Constitution [except] in the dependent clause of a sentence that has as its main point that students should ponder the paradox that the Constitution side-tracked the movement to abolish slavery." — Wall Street Journal, October 20, 1994

In that context, it's now open season. It's "Goals 2000" plus 3 1/2 years. All's fair in politics and hand grenades. We stand on the brink of the nastiest year in our history, so before we get completely sidetracked, I give the following grades, if you will, to various segments of our Society for the past year:

The "A" is the easiest grade to award. It goes to the American soldier. According to our Judeo-Christian Heritage, Joshua was told, "Every place that the soles of your feet shall trod upon, that have I given unto you, from this Lebanon even unto the great river, the river Euphrates." So far as I know as a layman, that promise was never completely fulfilled by any peoples except by the Brits earlier, and by the coalition in 2003. Our common foot soldiers have exhibited a kind of "faith and courage" the rest of us can only wonder if we could copy.

The "B" goes to President George W. Bush. Not to be presumptuous, but even he, when listing his Administration's accomplishments, doesn't seem to mention his involvement with the CFR, the Campaign Finance "Reform." BY THE WAY, if YOUR friends are selling "access" for DOLLAR BILLS, I'm sorry to hear about YOUR friends! My father was invited to the 1980 inaugural ball on the basis of a $10 "campaign contribution" (though he couldn't afford to attend).

A family member, however, recently achieved the destination by attending a White House "briefing" and having face-to-face "discussions" with the President's right hand man and some cabinet members. It didn't "cost" a cent, either, except participation in a citizens' group — which used to be considered "citizenship" or "civic duty"! The Left complains that the reason they can't teach kids to read is because they can't even get parents to attend a PTA meeting — which is a sorry excuse, because THEY taught those parents in the public schools! Evidently, instilling "civic duty" in those years wasn't a PRIORITY!

Subsequently, I must give the "republican" Congress a "C" for 2003. Their spending habits are giving drunken sailors a bad name. I don't claim that as an original thought because, if you're reading this, you've probably had the same thought yourself.

The "D" goes to the mainstream news media and most of the clergy who label themselves "mainstream"! It's a generous "D-minus" (only because they, on occasion, do something right)!

The "F," of course, goes to the entertainment media and the more leftist members of the "Loyal Opposition." I say of course because the F-word is their favorite word. Those candidates are typified by ROY G. BIV (a colorful personality), W.D. DIM (whose motto is "What difference does it make?"), and QWERTY UIOP, the alpha-alpha male (a cousin to Alley Oop, the Neanderthal).

To the general "populace" I must give an "INCOMPLETE"! Too much cutting of classes such as current events, history, and religion — in favor of the boob tubes and the baser pursuits such as pleasure and poppycock (wine, women, and thong).

We used to raise sheep, and there's a reason they're called DUMB sheep: when forced to make a decision, they can't decide which way to go until they figure out which way all the OTHERS are going to go, and then they instantly go that way with much exuberance! The sheep are sleeping off their holiday dinners, but will soon be asked to make decisions concerning the office of alpha-sheep.

Oh and I almost forgot the most obvious grade I have to give out: to the educational Establishment I award "SUSPENSION" (I was going to say "expulsion" but I didn't do it)! What they're doing to our children is almost criminal. Suspension is too good for most of our over-educated "ignoramousi." I'm not talking about good teachers in the grassroots; as someone once said, education is crucial if we are to avoid taking educated people seriously!

I paraphrase, but according to Mrs. Cheney, in 1992 the Federal government put 1.4 million dollars toward establishing "standards" as to what students should be taught about history. The grantee was the National Center for History in the Schools at UCLA. In its document-produced-by-committee, Senator Joseph McCarthy is mentioned 19 times, the KKK 17 times, and the Great Emancipator once (Paul Revere and the Wright brothers, not even once).

Thus we can pinpoint 1992 as the year Academia came out of its closet of subtlety forever. Classic oratory of the "great debates" of our history were ignored, except that students were urged to "analyze" Pat Buchanan's "culture war" speech at the Republican convention that year. Western civilization was "iced out" (as was, it goes without saying, the role of religion in American history).

Which reminds me of a dilemma: what grade to give the United Nations for 2003? The short answer is, the U.N.'s grade fell off the end of the curve somewhere at the end of the chart, just above abortionists, environmental extremists, and lawyers.

"But," some would ask, "how about a grade for Big Corporations?" The serious answer is, the jury is still out. Some of my best friends would remind me that money and power corrupt, to which I reply, "Everything corrupts these days." Even some conspiracy theories would corrupt you. Charlie Sykes, the radio host, once said, "Some people are more obsessed with making rich people poor than making poor people better off." This deserves its own column, but suffice it to say that money is a terrible master but an excellent servant.

This column's longer than usual, but you know, "if I can just help one person, it will be worth it." The thread running through this is Faith vs. The Thing We Feared the Most. There's a new twist to the joke about pessimism vs. optimism; the optimists now are trying to learn how to communicate with the animals and the pessimists are trying to find life on Mars (I saw it when it was close to the earth last summer, and it's obvious that there isn't any).

So finally, I just want to salute two men who "left us" this year: Bob Hope and a World War II veteran. The former is better remembered, but the latter is Warren Spahn, who survived four years as a combat soldier to go on to pitch 382 complete games in the major leagues against the likes of Mickey Mantle and Willie Mays. By the way, Spahn once played pro baseball for $60 a month, I understand (think about it, bud)!

One thing we can do is pray that today's veterans could come home to such a bright future, but don't bet the farm system on it. Only time, as man counts time, will tell!

James Monroe said, "While then [America] retains its sound and healthful state, everything will be safe. They will choose competent and faithful representatives for every department. It is only when the people become ignorant and corrupt, when they degenerate into a populace, that they are incapable of exercising the sovereignty. Usurpation is then an easy attainment and an usurper soon found: *the people themselves become the willing instruments of their own debasement and ruin.*"

Marilyn Monroe gets six pages in some "social science" textbooks, but who in the world was James Monroe?

The latest diet: DESSERTS can save your life!

January 2, 2004

"Never look back." —Satchel Paige

"Unless there's a runner on second base." —Curtis Dahlgren

When the clock struck 12 on New Year's Eve, where was your mind and what were you thinking? Were you thinking about the Californians who lost their homes last year? Or about tens of thousands of Iranians who lost both their homes and their lives? Or how about the one million Americans who were either buried in landfills or burned in incinerators last year (labeled as "Medical Waste")? I'm talking about the babies who were intentionally *killed in their own afterbirth before the fact* — "interruption of pregnancy" — "turn out the lights; the party's over!"

Probably not, because a lot of people, while adding to their waistlines, were thinking about nothing more than the latest lottery and "Why not me?" Very, very, few people were thinking about the reason they were born instead of aborted. There's a divine purpose for every human, for every "fetus" in fact, but few are aware of it. In my daily "readings" is this little poem:
There are a number of us who creep
Into the world, to eat and sleep,
And know no reason why we're born
Save only to consume the corn,

> Devour the cattle flock and fish,
> And leave behind an empty dish.

That happens to be the reading for "September 11th." But the word for the week is "desserts," which comes from a French word meaning, literally, "un-serve" or "clear the table." And I once gave a speech, "Desserts Can Save Your Life," that goes something like this:

Utopians look for differences and "inequities" and then look for scapegoats. Realists know that real progress is only made on a case-by-case, individual basis without alibis or excuses. To boil down what I'm saying to its quintessential parts, let's first dissect the word STRESSED:

> S= self-centeredness
> T= thanklessness
> R= rationalization
> E= emotionalism
> S= society (pop culture)
> S= Satan (2/3 of us believe he exists)
> E= envy
> D= defeat (and ultimate death)

ON THE OTHER HAND, THERE IS ANOTHER HAND:

> D= dedication (commitment to something Higher than man)
> E= enthusiasm (that word means God-in-us)
> S= spiritual-mindedness
> S= substance-over-symbolism
> E= expectations (Faith)
> R= responsibility
> T= Truth
> S= SUCCESS (and ultimate salvation)!

Therefore, "DESSERTS CAN save your life!"

Speaking of the lottery, there's a story about a man who prayed every day of his life, "Please, help me win the lottery; please, please, please!" Then one day the sky opened up like a curtain and a trumpet sounded a deafening blast, and a Voice boomed out, "Buy a TICKET!!"

I don't actually advocate THAT, but must admit that there must be a lesson in that joke somewhere there. Too many people start the New Year thinking about lottery "megabucks" instead of looking for an organized, logical success program (whether spiritual or general). As I said, the root of the word "desserts" means "clear the table" and it's a cousin to the word "desert" (as in "just deserts").

To get right to the nitty-gritty, the bottom-line question here is, when God "runs the table," are you going to be behind the 8-ball, or maybe a cue-stick in His hand? The late Johnny Cash (?-2003) used to sing, "Because you're mine, I walk the Line." There's no week like the present one to resolve to do so.

When God clears the table, what will you leave behind, anyway? Torn-up lottery tickets? Gold bricks (paving blocks)? Or just an empty dish? The Psalmist said, "I will walk at liberty for I seek thy precepts!"

If you get the drift, say Amen.

Why not "zero tolerance" for illiteracy?

January 10, 2004

"If I say, I will speak thus and such, behold, I should 'offend' the generation of thy children." — King David

YOU GET THE PICTURE: so-called "political correctness" has been around for a long, long time. Those who WANT to be offended "will be offended"! Paradoxically, those who are the most ardent advocates of so-called "tolerance" actually have no **toleration** for the slightest "offense"! Those who can dish it out, just can't "take it."

Today's all-powerful alpha-victims are shaking some formerly unshakable institutions. In his dissent on the decision concerning high school football game prayers, Chief Justice William Rehnquist said, "Even more disturbing than its holding is the tone of the court's opinion. It bristles with hostility to all things religious in public life" [i.e., hostility in the name of "tolerance"]! The majority's rationale was, in effect, "If we don't ban prayers, someone out there somewhere *might be offended!*" [the General Welfare Clause of the Constitution notwithstanding].

One of the dirty little secrets of American history is that our Founding Fathers didn't waste any time at all worrying whether their words would somehow "offend" an atheist. Thomas Jefferson said that there were a million believers for every non-believer. Lately, however, the offended-victim/litigation complex has become a growth industry almost as powerful as the military-industrial complex. School textbooks have replaced "Founding Fathers" with *"founders" (and only mentions them as scoundrels).*

We are rapidly losing all sense of the distinction between real and imagined "offenses." A first grader is expelled for "touching a skirt," but no one is "offended" that neither he nor the girl knows how to READ! I for one am insulted by the claim that in today's society, learning to read is so "complex" and so "difficult."

DISCLAIMER: If the following paragraphs are misconstrued as "teacher bashing," as my mother used to say, "Excuse me for living!" She once volunteered to read to kids in our local public school, though when I was a kid, no one ever "read to" us! WE read to the TEACHER. From the first day of kindergarten, we started learning the letters and reading them back to the teacher! Kindergarten in those days lasted six whole weeks, and by the end of it we were reading (English even, whether that was our parents' "first" language or not). The phrase "unable to read" hadn't been invented yet, and it never would have even occurred to us that someday kids would be given diplomas that they couldn't read!

However, the 12/28/03 Chicago Tribune page one headline reports, "State tosses 80,000 tests — Move inflates achievement scores at nearly 1,400 schools"! A small percentage of the "invalidations" were for legal technicalities, but the rest are "under investigation." Los Angeles and Houston, among other cities, have seen similar reports.

I wasn't born yesterday. It doesn't take a genius to smell a rat here. In order to try to keep "federal funds," one high school in Chicago had more than 92 per cent of its reading and math scores tossed out. And that's just based on the kids who stayed in school; I suspect that our "top people" in education are secretly glad that many drop out (as those kids would only drag the test score averages down even more).

To add insult to injury, the 01/04/04 Sunday Tribune page one headline says, "Critics: Tests dumb down math — Too much emphasis on basic skills, top educators say"! We used to hear the same argument about the basics in reading methods. Why? Evidently, in the attempt to devise mass-production, assembly-line techniques for teaching, the "basics" just require too much EFFORT.

This past week, I heard Dan Rather talk about the issue of tossed-out test scores, and incredibly, he tried to blame the President's Secretary of Education, and said he fears "the messenger" will be attacked. Ha! The only "grief" the media will get for reporting the story will come from the teachers' unions.

Teacher bashing? WHO is bashing WHOM? I think the inner-city *children* are the ones getting "bashed" here! My main problem is with the education departments at our institutions of "Higher Learning," not teachers in the trenches. Faddishly "innovative" teaching methods are the main obstacles, and lots of teachers don't even LIKE those methods. Also, local school boards and superintendents have some accountability (if they don't, they might as well be abolished).

A friend says my last column sounded "angry and harsh" ("DESSERTS Can Save Your Life"). I said that was mild compared to the NEXT one! I wonder if our elites who promote PC **"tolerance"** understand that that word means, literally, **"bearing it"**? They **probably don't have a clue!** For most of my life I've just been an observer, but when it comes to educational illiteracy, **I just can't BEAR it anymore!**

No one starts a weekly column at the age of 61 just for the fun of it, or just to complain for the sake of complaining. The time has come — if it's not already "past due" — to ask our highly-paid public school officials, board members, and teachers to stop wasting our hard-earned tax dollars. How about a prairie fire? HOW ABOUT A ZERO TOLERANCE POLICY ON ILLITERACY? As one of our Founding "Fathers" put it, "If this be treason, may God make the most of it"!

Our "top educators" probably wouldn't know him from Eve and Adam, but please pass this column on to your friends. If they think it sounds "harsh," they can always sue me. Better yet, sue the *Chicago Tribune!*

Give us this day our daily "spin"?

January 16, 2004

"Man is a creature who lives, not upon bread alone, but principally by catchwords." — Robert Louis Stevenson

SOME OF MY BEST FRIENDS are offended by my writing. Even quoting the Founding Fathers is considered too "political" and/or too "pro-republican" (with a small "r"). Hey, I didn't even keep the religion I was born with, so don't accuse me of being a "dyed-in-the-wool" ANYTHING!

I've never been a card-carrying Republican, but I did once belong to a union. The union's publication for members was called **The Line**. I never had a quarrel with them, but it just struck me as rather amusing — that title. People who adhere to group-speak — or their "LINE" — come hell or high water, are the real dyed-in-the-wool sheep. Pat answers and catchwords replace thinking outside the sheepfold.

Years before the term "political correctness" was coined, there appeared a prophetic article entitled **"Moral Dishonesty"** (*National Review, 12/19/75*). The author, Gerhart Niemeyer, said in the opening paragraph:

"A sensational book by the German paleontologist Heinrich Erben maintains that mankind is probably a declining species. He points to certain parallels between extinct animal species that lost their fitness for survival because they were too protected by circumstances, and the human race as it exists today . . . To Erben's list of human immaturities . . let us add another: moral dishonesty."

Niemeyer goes on to say, "In thinking about detente we tend to see the Soviet regime as a normal government, its relations to its subjects as normal policies [etc] . . . even though there is much evidence that says, It just ain't no. Evidence disturbing to attitudes of good will toward the Soviet Union is simply read out of court . . . The truth is conceived as an enemy of international goodness . . .

"Self-will may govern our actions but it does not sit easy in our souls. Moral dishonesty, by contrast, not only considers itself guiltless but positively glows in self-righteousness while heaping moral condemnation on those who disagree . . . Reason takes second place not to traditional morality but to subjective 'moral' intentions and the emotional self-satisfaction of supporting a public cause seen as progressive . . .

"Traditional morality — either the Ten Commandments, Aristotle's list of virtues, or Christ's double love of God and neighbor — can never pass off falsehood as the necessary price of goodness. That possibility belongs exclusively to modern progressivism . . . More than Tartuffe, who knew that he was lying, they suppress reason *by not allowing the voice of Truth to be heard even within their own hearts. A fraud of secular piety wholly engulfs their being, so that reason is dethroned . . .*

"It goes without saying that in the process not merely reason but morality itself is lost. For where reason and knowledge are despised, there Mephistopheles can easily snare Faust in the net of hell." [my emphasis]

All I can say is "WOW," to that! Hats off to that *National Review* from 1975, and I hope someone reminds them about that article. Nearly 30 years later, the "number one issues" may have changed, but the principles governing "mainstream conventional wisdom" — or Political Correctness — have not. There are many deceivers running "to and fro" in the world, and the main tool they all use is the catchword and/or, the catchphrase!

As a P.R. weapon, catchwords tend to be overused and lose effectiveness over time. Undaunted, the deceivers just shift gears and try new ones (please take note: their truthfulness is irrelevant and the only thing that matters is the effectiveness of the phrase for the progressive agenda)! Here are some of the more prominent ones that I recall, decade-by-decade:

In the 1950s, we often heard "witch-hunt" and "repression," and the biggest one in the colleges and universities was "value judgments" (as in, We must not make *value judgments* "because that produces repression and guilt").

In the smoking sixties, the main catchword was "revolution," and in the 70s it was "CHOICE"! During the roaring 80s, it was "multiculturalism," and, during the gay NINETIES, it was **hated** and/or **extremism.**

Evidently, those were going over like a lead balloon, because the Left is now trying a new tack: **"divisiveness"!!** If one "sighs and cries" about revolutionary federal court decisions, we are being "divisive" (but the activist judges usurping legislative powers, states' rights, and the Constitution itself, apparently, are promoting "harmony" I guess)!

Another catchword is **"special interest group."** The right to petition government and freedom of speech were just "read out of court" last month (McCain-Feingold). Speech on behalf of unborn babies can now be outlawed during an election, as written anti-slavery speech was forbidden in the mails from 1835 to 1844. The abolitionists were, of course, a **"special interest group"**!

It's no wonder that the so-called "pro-choicers" want to shut up certain "special interest groups" — because **babies ARE special!**

One of this year's candidates for President was asked what his favorite New Testament book was, and he said "Job" but he "didn't like the ending"! If he didn't like the way that one ended, he certainly isn't going to like "the ending" of that other one, Revelation!

And he ought to read that other New Testament author, Isaiah, who talked about our "turning things upside down" and putting "sweet for bitter and bitter for sweet," calling good "evil" and evil "good." I don't care if we do have a remote-controlled car running around the surface of Mars, man is a declining species.

Judging by the national news coverage of the Northeastern cold snap today, it sounds like the nanny state and the entitlement mentality are beginning to extend to the weather. Which reminds me: global warming is one of those subjects similar to the old Soviet Union — in that the "accepted" opinions must not be even questioned. **"Global warming" is the ultimate catchphrase, and catchwords "rule." Even on the coldest night of the year!**

Shades of Cincinnatus: a "farmer's" State of the Union message

January 20, 2004

"Just because you do not take an interest in politics doesn't mean that politics won't take an interest in you." - Pericles

JUST ASK THE "CITIZENS" OF THE SIBERIAN GULAG (1920-something to about 1989). In a new book by Anne Applebaum (GULAG, A REPORT, Doubleday), a woman is quoted: "Before my arrest, I led an ordinary life, typical of a professional Soviet woman who didn't belong to the Party. I worked hard but took no particular part in politics or public affairs. My real interests lay with home and family." —Chicago Tribune, 1/04/04, Books (Michael Marrus)

No living historian can tell us for sure how many such "working people" the politicians had taken an "interest" in, and who were sent to their deaths in Siberia or other slave labor camps ranging from the Arctic circle to the suburbs of Leningrad to Kazakhstan. "Depending on how and who one counts, and including the executed and non-Soviets," the dead may have numbered 10, 12, or even 20 million. I alluded to this in my last column, but didn't mean to just skim over it.

Having said that, let's back up a bit further. In baseball, a runner never backtracks unless he thinks he might have missed a base, so I wanted to go back and touch a couple of bases. One such topic is the weather. Despite the current political climate, the networks and the people really seem to want to talk about the weather, especially if it's cold. So:

The Entitlement mentality seems to be extending to the weather, and I think I'm on to something. I'm writing these words before the President's State of the Union address, and someone said this morning that President Ford may have been the only President to give an objective one (he essentially said we could be doing better). Now earlier the President proposed some kind of a "grain bank" in case of world hunger.

I know, I know, at the present time we Americans are so hard up for something to complain about that people are "offended" over school nicknames, and will sue at the drop of a coffee cup, but I think the President had something there. I know that a long, hot summer is the last thing on your mind right now, but just bear with me. While many of you are fantasizing about going south and "catching some rays," we Yoopers fantasize about a world that's "whiter than snow" (a tad like Siberia but without the blood and tears).

A big-city TV weather-guy once started to say something about "pretty" snow, but he caught himself and said, "People get upset when I call it pretty!" I once saw a book of cartoons called "Who Invented Rain?" In it, a little boy saying his prayers says, "Maybe people would like snow better if you made more than one flavor."

Another little boy says, "I wish God wouldn't wash the world on Saturday." Historians and anthropologists can tell a lot about a civilization by the things the people laugh about. Only one per cent of our population now lives on the farm and we've stopped praying "Give us this day our daily bread" because we think that's a "given." Kids in high school now are too young to remember the 1988 drought.

I made a cross-country trip in the spring of 1989 from dry San Diego through the drier Yuma, Arizona desert and the Texas Panhandle. As I beheld the brittle grass, driving across Kansas, I heard the following lyrics on the radio:

As long as there's a rainbow, there's a reason for the rain.

If we're ever going to see a rainbow, we can stand a little rain.

I'm no stranger to the rain; I can spot bad weather, but I'll put this cloud behind me.

In eastern Kansas, I heard two county agents being interviewed. One from Phillips County, up on the Nebraska line, said: "I've lived here almost a year now and I haven't seen it rain yet." Yet the very same day, I pulled in a Chicago station and the announcer said, "It's going to be 50 degrees on Saturday and even warmer Sunday, BUT WE MAY HAVE TO PUT UP WITH A LITTLE RAIN"(!)

If you city dudes have never heard the facts of life, let me clue you in. In 1989, Miami got 42 inches of rain, including a deluge during one football game, but the four counties in south Florida ended the year under strict water-use regulations because the "normal" amount is 56 inches. Now, to get 56 inches in a year, they probably need at least two good rains per week, and mathematically speaking, that means on average 4 chances out of 7, or a 56% chance, of getting rain on at least one of the days <u>on the weekend!</u>

During the 1988 drought, on a Friday night, I heard a Wisconsin weatherman say, "There are a few clouds in northern Indiana, but it's **nothing to worry about!**" And during the same period a rock station DJ said, "It's going to be a <u>beautiful</u> day out in the Plains, except for **a few pesky showers.**"

Evidently, that county agent from Phillips County never got to see those **pesky showers!** On June 11, 1988, disc jockeys all over the dial were raving about the "magnificent" and "fantastic" weather — 13 percent humidity and 20 mph winds! If we were ever to experience a repeat of 1988, those city folks would run plum out of adjectives! Funny thing is, that 99% who don't live on farms would be the *first* to run out of food, **not the last!**

Maybe people would like rain better if God had made more than one flavor. Hmmmm: maybe if He put a little booze in it . .
.

But what in tarnation does this have to do with the State of the Union? Well, Alan Keyes says that our future does not depend on our leaders. It depends on us. Truly said, but the more and more urbanized we become, the more I'm worried about the **people!** If you're still going "What's your point?" — then I know I'm really on to something here.

We're not going to have a "Great Society" or "New Frontiers" on the moon and Mars if we can't first get back to the basics. That's more than just a catchphrase with me. I grew up milking cows and I'm back to milking cows. I know which side our "guns" are buttered on.

Cincinnatus was a farmer who happened to be a Roman Senator during the days of the decline and fall. He tried his best to give wisdom to the Senate, and I wonder what advice he would have for our President today. One thing you can probably be sure of is that he would say, "Don't try to please EVERYBODY!" I don't think Cincinnatus would be a big fan of "triangulation"!

I heard a parable about an old man who was leading a donkey with a little boy riding the donkey. People shook their heads and said, "Look at that boy making that old man walk" so they traded places. Then people shook their heads and said, "Look at that man making that poor boy walk!"

So they decided to try a third way: lead the donkey with two ropes. And the donkey spooked on a mountain trail and pulled them both off the cliff.

Will the real Thomas Jefferson please STAND UP?

January 28, 2004

"History is more or less bunk." — Henry Ford

Let's play "What's My Line?" Contestant #1 says, "My name is Tom Jefferson and I was a Deist." Contestant #2 says, "My name is Tom Jefferson and I was a secular philosopher of the Enlightenment." Contestant #3 says, "My name is Tom Jefferson and I was a pioneer lawyer in the Freedom from religion movement."

Our panel of "experts" says: "All of the above!" SURVEY SEZ: "The 'experts' must know what they're talking about, right?" But would "You Bet Your Life," or even your De Soto, on that? GONG! Better NOT!

The magic word for the day is **bunkum;** say the magic word and you get a gold star. The "Jefferson" described above is a fictional character who never existed. Our friendly local purveyors of social "science" have swallowed a **line** — hook, bait, and bobber. They were fed that "line" in college and now we're all being taken for a ride, as in "Jump in, hang on, and shut up." But there is a right answer to the question, "Whom was the real Thomas Jefferson?" Facts, as someone once said, are stubborn things.

The awkward "trivia" fact for those who teach our teachers is: Jefferson left behind 18,000 public and private letters that we know of, plus his official speeches and papers. With all that evidence, how could so many, for so long, be so wrong? I hate to have to be the one to burst the bubble, but here's just a small sample of Jefferson's actions as President of the United States:

- He attended religious services in the Capitol Building (and such services were also held in the Supreme Court building)!
- He favored using the word "God" in the national motto!
- He granted land, buildings, and salaries for clergy teaching in Indian schools!
- Supported the use of the Bible as reading materials in such schools!
- He personally prayed at public events!
- Exempted churches from taxation!
- In 1801, he wrote that "the Christian religion, when divested of the rags in which [the clergy] have enveloped it, is a religion of all others most friendly to liberty, science, and freest expansion of the human mind." *

Sorry about that, Annie. The Freedom From Religion Foundation and ACLU keep bouncing back and forth between saying it is impossible to know the "original intent" of the Founders but then quoting them when such quotes can be twisted to appear to support their agenda. On the one hand, they and their lawyers, with the support of the news media, use early Jeffersonian quotes — and quotes from his enemies during his political campaigns — while trying to keep a lid on later Jefferson thoughts with the other hand.

Certainly he read philosophers such as Plato (he read everything, but he didn't like Plato). But he also read the Bible in four languages! He was only 33 years old when he wrote the Declaration of Independence, and over the next 50 years (it should go without saying) his view of the universe had been "evolved" and fine-tuned! After losing a wife and daughter, and approaching the end of his own life, his letters took on a "new tone."

One of his biographers, who spent over 50 years studying Jefferson the man, said that when he was young he thought he would someday know Jefferson completely. But that in the end, he didn't think anyone in this life would ever really know Jefferson. That makes it all the more outrageous when latter-day "historians" dogmatically claim to "know" that he was a Deist or an advocate of absolute "separation" of religion and state!

Deists believed in a hands-off God, a world without miracles; **Jefferson thought America was a miracle!** Most of the clergy called him an infidel when he ran for President, but Jefferson would be dumbfounded to wake up and discover that one letter out of 18,000 is now being used to try to "cleanse" the public square, and the marketplace of ideas, of religion (that Virginia's Freedom OF Religion is now being stood on its head as public "Freedom FROM Religion")!

Jefferson had us pegged from the beginning though. As were the rest of the Founders, he was realistic about human nature, and once said that from the conclusion of this [Revolutionary] war, "we will be going down hill." To the orthodox Left, virtue is repulsive, so one's self-esteem can only be enhanced by poking holes in the armor of our heroes, with shoddy and very shallow scholarship.

In the old days, even orphans had a role model, the "father of our country." Those of us who went to the "old school" always knew that Washington was a virtuous man with or without the "cherry tree" story. The evidence was there, but the New Age schools are using the cherry tree story as the excuse to toss out 22 million volumes of evidence about our forebears from the Library of Congress (figuratively speaking)! And some of the schools that were named for Washington have even changed their names!

There will be *consequences* for this wild joy ride by our educators. Lincoln once said that those who twist history have **"no right to mislead others, who have less access to history, and less leisure to study it, into [a] false belief . . . "** Teddy Roosevelt also has a quote about those who intentionally "mislead" others in the name of obtaining *leadership* during a political campaign.

77

John Adams' last words were, "Jefferson still lives." He didn't know that Jefferson had died earlier on the same day, July 4, 1826, but his words are prophetic. Lincoln said, "Soberly, it is now no child's play to save the principles of Jefferson from total overthrow in this nation"!

The same goes for January 2004, and this isn't just an intellectual jousting match among eggheads, nor a game that politicians and judges play. There are consequences out in the real world, intended or not intended!

As I said, boys and girls, the word for the day is *"bunkum."* Back in the 1820s, there was a congressman from Buncombe County, North Carolina and one day he gave an extremely long and boring, meaningless to the business at hand, speech in Congress. He explained to his colleagues later that he was only "speaking to Buncombe." Thus originated Henry Ford's term, **bunk** (short for "Buncombe").

In the "soft sciences" in our colleges and universities today, much of what passes for "knowledge" is just subjective bunk aimed at pleasing one's professor and/or graduate teacher, who in turn is just trying to please his department head, who may be just trying to please some new theory out there in the **pop** *culture (i.e., Buncombe).*

P.S. On the eve of the anniversary of Roe v. Wade, a Sheboygan woman gave birth in the bathroom stall at work, stuffed tampon flaps into the baby's mouth to shut it up, and put it, in a plastic bag, into her locker. She then went back to work without even wondering if it was a "she" or a "boy." The police found the baby girl frozen solid in the woman's car trunk, but in the end she may be punished less than someone who kills a cat, because if she had "aborted" the baby a day earlier she would have been a "heroine" to the pop culture. Welcome to the "age of tolerance"!

If you think our Founding Fathers would "sit down and shut up,"

while the Freedom they lived and died and bled for is now being invoked in the name of such grisliness and narcissistic depravity, you are full of **BUNK!**

* Footnote: facts in this column came from *The Real Thomas Jefferson* by Maxwell, et al (quoted by D. James Kennedy), *Christianity and the Constitution, the Faith of Our Founding Fathers* by John Eidsmoe (Baker Books, Grand Rapids MI), and other documented sources.

Abraham, Justin, and John . . .

February 3, 2004

"Right or wrong, God judge me not man. For be my motive good or bad, of one thing I am sure . . . lasting condemnation."
—*John Wilkes Booth (letter to President Lincoln, 1864)*

Talk about "a failure of intelligence"! Not just a failure to protect the President, but a failure of Confederate IQs in not being able to foresee either the consequences of seizing Union property before Lincoln's inauguration, or the further results of assassinating the President.

Was the "real" Abraham Lincoln a "trigger happy" Barry Goldwater (as portrayed on TV in 1964)? Long before March 4, 1861, the Confederacy had begun overrunning its headlights. They were tone deaf and color blind to the difference between "perception" and reality. Two weeks before the inauguration, General Beauregard had resigned as superintendent of West Point and placed shore batteries opposite Fort Sumter in Charleston harbor.

The curtain was about to be drawn on the drama that was to include Booth's final act. The perception was, as Booth's letter said, "The very nomination of Abraham Lincoln, four years ago, spoke plainly of war . . . His election proved it."

One of Abe's opening lines was, "If it were admitted that you who are dissatisfied hold the right side in the dispute, there is no single good reason for precipitate action. Intelligence, patriotism, Christianity, and a firm reliance on Him who has never forsaken this favored land, are still competent to adjust in the best way all our present difficulty."

Booth says: "Await an overt act? Till we are bound and plundered? What folly!"

But like the Old Testament prophets, Lincoln had framed the situation correctly: not *us versus them*, but all of us *versus the Almighty One*. "Suppose you go to war, you cannot fight always; and when after much loss on both sides, and no gain on either, you cease fighting, the identical old questions as to terms of intercourse are again upon you."

A guest at the Inaugural Ball found it a "melancholy function," and saw in Lincoln's "plain, ploughed face" the same "sense of becoming educated and needing education" that pained him. Toward such an end I dedicate this review of the drama. Twenty-first century America has grave issues pregnant with consequences, too. We could use some of the wisdom of history, but most of us get our "history" in bits and pieces from our parents and our peers, not the original sources.

Apologists for Booth say that he had a fear of scarring his pretty face, but the paradox is, he and his friends had MADE Lincoln the future President back in 1857 — when he was nothing but a homely, chronic loser living in Springfield, Illinois. If Davis and Lee, et al, had been as smart as advertised, perhaps cooler heads with a little foresight could have rewritten the whole script.

The South's fatal **gambit** happened more than three years before Lincoln arrived in Washington. It happened because hotter heads made a decision that split the Democrat Party right down the middle — at the very moment it was at its zenith, in control of the White House, Congress, and the Supreme Court (Dred Scott).

Against the warnings of many southern newspapers, they insisted upon making the prospective state of Kansas a slave state come hell or high water. We got the former, because even Senator Douglas was forced to break with his own President, Buchanan (which helped Douglas defeat Lincoln in 1858). But the southern Democrats, themselves, had made Lincoln the thing he became, "the thing they feared the most"!

The following excerpts are from *America in 1857, a Nation on the Brink* by Kenneth M. Stampp (Oxford University Press):

"A Massachusetts editor believed that Buchanan might have broken the Republican party and made his own party unbeatable in the North if he had honored his commitment to a fair vote on the Kansas constitution. Instead . . . he mistakenly gambled that the northern [Democrats] would submit even to the Lecompton fraud [a vote tilted by illegal Missouri voters crossing into the Territory] . . .

"The *Mobile Register* called the Kansas controversy 'pregnant with consequences' [and] 'The South never made a worse move,' wrote the angry editor of the Louisville Democrat at the end of 1857. 'A blunder, it is said, is worse than a crime; but this is both a blunder and a crime.'"

The generally pro-slavery *Richmond Enquirer* correctly predicted that trying to force northern Democrats to support the extension of slavery to the Territories would be suicidal, and would in effect guarantee the election of a Republican President in 1860. "By 1857 . . . with a substantial free-state majority already there, and with a host of northern emigrants expected to arrive that spring and summer, THE OUTCOME OF THE KANSAS CONTROVERSY SHOULD HAVE BEEN CLEAR ENOUGH." — ibid

So? Well, this is the time of year the fans of the old, OLD South like to rip Lincoln on the Internet forums, calling him everything from "tyrant" to destroyer of the Constitution. I've given up trying to answer them directly, but there IS an answer. My mother taught me the power of the "dumb question" asked at just the right time, so here are a few "dumb" questions for the Lincoln haters:

— How come they never complained about the Gag Rules of 1835-44 (that was a case of Federal meddling the South just loved, outlawing abolitionist literature in the mail)?

— What about the wolves across the Atlantic who were *praying* for a divided America?

— Would we be living under Nazi German rule today if the Rebellion had "succeeded"?

— Once elected, what was Lincoln supposed to do — refuse to take the job?

— Since when, does sending reinforcements to protect the lives of U.S. soldiers equate with an "overt act of war" (Fort Sumter)?

— Don't like the suspension of Habeas Corpus? There was a Revolution going on; what did you EXPECT to happen?

— Don't like what happened after the war? Did you think that assassinating Lincoln would HELP the situation?

— What was the role of sin in causing the Civil War, including the nation's sins of omission (England had solved its "slavery problem" without a Civil War)?

Robert E. Lee had said before war broke out that the Constitution had no provision for secession, and he didn't think the South had sufficient grounds for a Revolution. However, he would fight for Virginia no matter which side it came down on. The Civil War is a fairly "complex" topic, but the lowest common denominator is **human nature.** Churchill said that democracy was the worst form of *human* government, "except for all the others."

But Thomas Jefferson said of Christ: "He pushed His scrutinies into the heart of man, erected His tribunal in the region of his thoughts, and purified the waters at the fountainhead. He taught emphatically the doctrines of a future state [the Kingdom] . . . and wielded it with efficacy as an important incentive, supplementary to the other motives to moral conduct."

Translation: emotions are to be ruled by the mind and the "fountainhead"! One of Lincoln's lines from the opening act was: "Though passion may have strained, it must not break our bonds of affection. The mystic chords of memory, stretching from every battle-field and patriot grave to every heart and hearthstone all over this broad land, will yet swell the chorus of the Union when again touched, as surely they will be, by the better angels of our nature."

"Then" [writes Carl Sandburg, quoted by Paul Angle in *The Lincoln Reader*] "stepped forward Chief Justice Taney, worn, shrunken, odd, with 'the face of a galvanized corpse' . . . His hands shook with age, emotion, both, as he held out an open Bible toward the ninth President to be sworn in by him." Justice Taney had voted with the majority in Dred Scott, dehumanizing black people below the Mason-Dixon line. Maybe that's the reason his hands were shaking.

On that Bible, Lincoln did solemnly promise to defend the Constitution of the United States of America. I hope I can continue this story some time, but consider this a pre-emptive strike for Truth, before our academicians start to "dis-myth" Lincoln the way they've "debunked" the 18th century Patriots.

P.S. That reminds me about the Super Bowl. I probably could have offended fewer people today if I had just talked about football. I could have talked about sex-for-football-recruits at a Western university, which would have fit right in with my recent criticism of "Higher Education" in general. Or I could have talked about the Super Bowl half-time "show-and-tell." The word for the day, boys and girls, is *no comment*.

Nevertheless, let me just say one thing about that: If Rush Limbaugh's hand had ever come within two feet of a woman's breast at a football game on national TV, Rush would probably be in leg irons and stocks in the town square today. The "dirty dancing" pair should confess they planned the whole thing or else the miss should press charges of assault against the perpetrator. Call me square, but as long as the double standard exists, boycotting LaLa Land is the only logical thing to do.

John Wilkes Booth wasn't the last actor to ever try to "make history"! And as he says, in the final line of our script, "God judge me."

From "mystical memories" to high-tech trash: America, please phone home!

February 11, 2004

". . . appealing to the Supreme Judge of the world for the rectitude of our intentions . . . " —John Hancock, et al

IT'S A "MYSTERY" TO HER, says Senator Clinton, what was so good about the olden days (I paraphrase). Of all people, she ought to have a clue about that, but habitual revisionism seems to hide the obvious from modern eyes. They just can't handle a *paradox* well.

Not to make this totally personal, but I attended school from the late 40s through the 50s and on and off during the 60s and 70s, so I have some obvious basic Truths etched into my memory. One thing we could say for sure about our one-room country school is that we never pretended that education must always be "fun," or that "self-esteem" was our Holy Grail.

The paradox is, however, that education WAS fun for us, because we all loved to read (which only incidentally produced plenty of self-esteem, even among those who would now have been called academically "challenged"). Personally, I probably would have been put on Ritalin by today's standards, but from the first day of kindergarten we learned how to sit still and listen — which included listening to grades 1-8 review their lessons.

Since even our primary readers contained stories about American history, my calculation is that I absorbed over 64 years of history before entering high school. And horror of horrors (!) the Bible society even passed out New Testaments to every kid in public school! **Analyze that,** if you want to be a critic.

Speaking of "Grammies," history was just a reality of life for my family, with all of my grandparents being born in the 1800s, my father just 74 years after the death of Thomas Jefferson and John Adams (it's a very young country yet). English was a second language for my mother and dad, and my mother's mother raised 13 children without the benefit of sex education, day care, or a career! She was what would now be described as a "fundamentalist extremist."

Her 13 kids nearly all had life-long marriages, which produced 56 or 57 productive citizens. The third-generation Americans, my generation, began to drift out into society's changing "mainstream," subsequently experiencing some problems never before known in the family. The fourth generation, it seems, is the one that usually begins to hit bottom. If I may generalize here, they drifted even further out into the mainstream and suffered everything from broken homes to child sexual abuse. (Surprahse, surprahse)

The year 1964 was a great turning point for the whole country. There was a Jenkin Lloyd Jones who used to write a column in which he would ask, "Have we reached the stomach-turning point yet?" We hadn't.

In the 70s, during a visit by some of my "5th generation" cousins, I was going to play "The Ten Commandments" movie in my Betamax. They didn't want to see it. I pointed out that it had won the Oscar for Best Picture when it came out. They still flatly refused to see it. Do you see a pattern here yet?

During the 40s, a local girl had been kidnapped and murdered, but that was probably the only murder in our county for 40 years.

These days, more people are murdered in NYC and Washington, DC every year than the number of soldiers killed in combat. With a touch of sarcasm, just before he died, Garner Ted Armstrong wrote, "Won't it be *wonderful* when Iraq is just like America?"

Life has become so cheap in America that the 12 million or so babies killed by "legal" and "safe" abortion from 1973 to 1985 were the equivalent of the population of 12 states: Oregon, Idaho, Montana, North Dakota, South Dakota, Wyoming, Utah, Nevada, New Mexico, Kansas, Nebraska, and Colorado. With about 45 million "safe" abortion deaths now, I don't know how many states that would equal.

"Shall I not visit for these things? saith the Lord; shall not my soul be avenged in a nation such as this?" As Jeremiah said, "A wonderful and horrible thing is committed in the land [in the Hebrew, 'a stunning and filthy thing']?"

And then we had the Super Bowl. "It's only a breast — what's the big deal?" says LaLa Land, which can't even sell a Civil War story without explicit sex. "What's the big deal?" Try asking that of the dead girl in Florida who was kidnapped two days after "Super Bowl Sunday." Try telling that to the dozens of victims of a Green Bay bar owner who were "allegedly" drugged, raped, and videotaped over the years. Try telling that to the Minnesota co-ed who is still missing and hasn't even had a decent burial (likewise, those 45 million babies).

But we DO have a radio-controlled car or 2, running around the planet Mars! Big deal! The man-made computer I'm writing on is awesome, but it doesn't thrill me half as much as seeing the design of the leaf of the ginkgo tree, or a sonogram of a baby sucking its thumb in the womb, or the scan of the human brain (that designed the computer). In a nutshell, that sums up how our world-view has been turned upside down since I was born (I was conceived before Pearl Harbor). Some of our kids would go, like, who was Pearl Harbor? **Time to turn over a new leaf?**

This could be the year my TV goes out to the dumpster. It may as well, for all I use it. Only three words are needed for a laugh on a sit-com: O MY GOD. One sit-com actress even said, "O MY

LIVING GOD!" and got a big laugh on the sound track. Four words — what's the big deal?

Well, MADAM, God's not quite dead yet, and I'm reminded of "The Religion of Abraham Lincoln," a book by William Wolf. He wrote of a conversation on religion in Lincoln's office in 1859. "Lincoln expressed himself in about these words . . . he understood punishment for sin to be a Bible doctrine; that the punishment was parental in its object, aim, and design, and intended for the good of the offender . . . He added this remark, that 'punishment being a provision of the gospel system, he was not sure but the world would be better off if a little more punishment was preached by our ministers, and not so much pardon of sin.'"

By the way, most of the ministers in Springfield voted against him when he ran for President. Many churches had turned the gospel into an "escape" for the next world while ignoring the present one (i.e., an "escape" from the **penalty** for sin, but not from the sin itself). You can't have both "worlds," or two masters.

I once wrote to the head of my former church that when Malachi wrote about turning the hearts of the fathers to the "children," that that includes our **unborn** children. He replied that the church had "never taught that"! Well, maybe it's **time to turn over a new leaf!**

Also, when Malachi spoke of turning the hearts of the "children" to the "fathers" — in the Hebrew, father (or *ab)* means, "father in a literal and immediate, **or** a figurative and remote sense" (i.e., *forefathers*).

In his farewell address to America, "the father of our country" (Washington) said - to future lawyers and courts: "Of all the dispositions and habits which lead to political prosperity, Religion and Morality are indispensable supports. In vain would that man claim the tribute of Patriotism who should labor to **subvert** these great pillars of human happiness . .

"Where is the security for property, for reputation, **for life,** if the sense of religious obligation desert the oaths which are the instrument of investigation in Courts of Justice? And let us indulge ["tolerate"] with caution the supposition that morality can be maintained without religion. Whatever may be conceded to the influence of refined education on minds of peculiar structure [a minority of people], **reason and experience** both forbid us to expect that national morality can prevail in exclusion of religious principle."

"Progressive humanists" now believe the opposite, that a four-year college education for everyone is the only thing needed to preserve us. And the last time I was in college, I told myself before classes started to prepare to hear my Judeo-Christian heritage attacked before the first week was out. My landscaping professor wasted no time. On the first day of class he "informed" us that the book of Genesis was to blame for all the "pollution" in the world, because it says "replenish the earth and SUBDUE it"!

The latest "60 Minutes" program tried to portray evangelicals in the same intolerant light, but there was an article in the Nov.-Dec. 99 issue of *The Humanist* entitled "The Trouble With Tolerance." J. Eric Hazell, a history professor, said: "Secular defenders of tolerance say, fine, believe in Jesus but don't try to impose your belief on me. But if you take the proselytizing out of evangelicalism — which is what advocates of tolerance desire — what are you tolerating? Not much."

The champions of "tolerance" are actually practicing a form of thought control, enforcing a "relativist" world-view. They want to drive all religion underground (except for Darwinism and/or "Eastern" religions that they try to "impose" on their captive audiences). However, a philosophy professor was recently forced to resign because he wasn't allowed to tell his students that he was a believer, which was simply where he was coming from! The culture war is thus a one-way street, and will be won by **forfeit** if we meekly turn over the arena of ideas to those who say, "Just trust us, believe us, and don't rock the boat!"

"The framers of the Constitution held no utopian dreams. They recognized with John Adams that human nature had not changed 'since the Garden of Eden,' and that there had been 'no improvement in morals since the days of Jesus.' The idea of upward evolutionary progress was foreign to them . . .

"A constitution is never a match for an immoral or ignorant people determined to trample on its provisions. But when properly enforced it can buy time for the nation." — excerpt from Christianity and the Constitution, the Faith of our Founding Fathers, John Eidsmoe.

Justice Felix Frankfurter said, "What governs is the Constitution, and not what we have written about it." Well, I almost got through 21 columns without bringing up the L-word. I avoid it as much as possible, because someday its definition will be restored to the "original intent." My 1938 Funk and Wagnalls says:

> *liberal*, *adjective*; *generous*; *plentiful, as a liberal gift, liberal abuse, or liberal harvest*

Look around you. We are seeing more liberal abuse than liberal harvests. This may be in part a failure to communicate, but what we have here is not a failure of just your political opponents, but a failure of what's in our **hearts.** Personally, I'm not the man my father was, and he probably wasn't the man *his* father was, but I'm at the stomach-turning point with having **OUR** basic beliefs portrayed by the media as extremism, hypocrisy, or even fascism!

Maybe I AM "trying to turn back the clock" (or at least trying to "buy some time for the nation"). A very wise man once said that God will keep His protecting hand over us as long as 51% of us are essentially trying to "do good" and be faithful to our spiritual forefathers.

Conclusion: There's a new book out, "God and Ronald Reagan, a spiritual life" by Paul Kengor. As quoted from *Newsmax* magazine (Feb. 04), one highlight is: "The turning point in Reagan's war with the Soviets was the emergence of Mikhail Gorbachev, who became the Soviet general secretary in 1986. Reagan thought Gorbachev was different. His frequent reference to God made Reagan believe that the Communist leader was a secret Christian.

After meeting Gorbachev, an excited Reagan told aide Michael Deaver, 'He believes'"!

Some "secret Christians" even keep it secret from God, of course, but leaving that aside, the bottom line is that what was in the hearts of those two men was, in the end, more significant than our military buildup or the threat of "Star Wars." Maybe this is a dumb question again, but "What's in your heart?"

P.S. Happy birthday, Charles Darwin. I'm not being entirely facetious, but at least I've said my piece. Now, if necessary, I could die in peace (at least if you will forward this for me to at least five lawyers and five newspapers).

America's nervous breakdown: Another legacy of the 60s

February 21, 2004

"An elective despotism is not the government we fought for." —Thomas Jefferson

"What is truth?" —Pontius Pilate

"What is IS?" —President Clinton

"Whatever!" —John Q. Public [paraphrasing]

IN HIS FIRST INAUGURAL ADDRESS, President Washington made a most significant statement. You ought to have some high school students read it today to see if they can make heads or tails out of it:

> There is no truth more thoroughly established than that there exists in the course of nature an indissoluble union between virtue and happiness [and] we ought to be no less persuaded that the propitious smiles of Heaven can never be expected on a nation that disregards the eternal rules of order and right which Heaven itself has ordained.

The concepts of "truth" and "virtue" would go right over the heads of many of our contemporary students, and most wouldn't be able to pronounce "indissoluble." I'm harping on public education again, but we can't get too much of that. I've met three graduates of a local high school who didn't even know what the 4th of July commemorates. I even had to explain what the word "commemorates" means, and when given a clue to the answer, "England," they all said the same thing: "The Beatles!"

In spite of the fact that the public schools are one of our tax system's largest budget items, the taxpayer's opinion is only scorned. Standardized tests are not wanted, period. The educational establishment not only doesn't want the current status of students to be measured but they most certainly DO NOT want expected future declines in basic academic skills to be quantified and chronicled (neither student scores, nor the teachers' scores).

It is no coincidence, but many of today's education school professors and local school administrators were hippie anti-establishmentarians back in the SIXTIES! Even some of our Presidents!

The following excerpt is from a 1999 column to the *L.A. Times:*

"The partisan bickering over Bill Clinton's scandal-engulfed presidency has obscured a far larger and more culturally significant battle . . The ostensible reason for President Clinton's impeachment is alleged perjury and obstruction of justice. The real issue, however, may be his 'embrace' of deconstruction in modern America.

"For decades, the theory of deconstruction has enjoyed a vogue in academe. It originated in linguistics, where, to oversimplify, it posited the none-too-radical idea that language was a function of shared meaning. In this view, a word had no objective meaning; it could only mean something because people agreed on its meaning.

"From linguistics, however, deconstruction passed into textual interpretation. Here, the idea was that a text — say, a novel [or the Constitution] — had no set meaning; it, too, was a collaboration between the writer and the reader . . . If deconstruction had confined itself to English departments, it might have served as just another analytical tool. But deconstructionists were rabid partisans who realized their theory had grave implications **not just for literature but for the very notion of reality. If nothing was objective . . . then the entire world was subjective . . .**

"When reality itself is a subjective construct, morality is also relative. There is no moral authority in the sky, no moral absolutes . . . In the longer view, the Clinton scandal not only raised the issue of deconstruction; it was the latest and fiercest battle in what we might now recognize as a long cultural civil war . . [The Left's] is no holy war. It is a gigantic therapy session in which everyone is allowed, in 1960s rhetoric, to do his or her own thing . . . **One suspects we will see people fall on their swords before they give up that fight.**" — "Why impeachment is a cultural, not a political battle" by Neal Gabler, quoted in the *Las Vegas Review-Journal*, January 7, 1999 (my emphasis)

Brings to mind an experience I had during the late 60s. The late semanticist (and later U.S. Senator), S.I. Hayakawa, was speaking at a big-city university and we had to run a gauntlet of "peace protestors" to get into the assembly hall. One of the men behind me asked the protestors, "Why don't you stick up for your country?"

"The world is my country," shot back the "student." I'll never forget the sinking feeling I got in the gut. I was shocked not only by the content of the words, but by the instantaneousness with which the reply came back. In its reflexivity, it was robotically automaton-like. The teachers of the New-World-Order had been "teaching our children well"! Teaching them to be America-haters first, without an original thought in their bones.

Fast-forward 30-something in years. We stand at the year 2004's probable high point. I think it's all down hill from here. It's time for the 2-minute drill, with only a minute left on the clock, a Catch-22 for my 22nd column. We're well-fed to the point of "fat," and no one seems to care very much that a New Autocracy of Raw Judicial Power has been unleashed on America, from seashore to shining seashore. The bell tolls clearly, and it tolls for thee, Columbia.

Even the so-called churches are silent for the most part. **One of the legacies of the 60s is "barometer Christians."** Many of them wanted to go to church immediately after 9/11 — **ONCE!** And they haven't been seen in church again. They are "moved" by great emotion, but too often off-put by Washington's kind of reason and logic.

I ask your indulgence, at this time, for some freely quoted excerpts from a speech by Senator Zell Miller last week in the Senate. He makes some of the same points I was going to make anyway:

A Deficit of Decency: "The Old Testament prophet Amos was a sheep herder who lived back in the Judean hills, away from the larger cities of Bethlehem and Jerusalem. Compared to the intellectual urbanites like Isaiah and Jeremiah, he was just an unsophisticated country hick.

"But Amos had a unique grasp of political and social issues and his poetic literary skill was among the best of all the prophets. That familiar quote of Martin Luther King, Jr. about 'Justice will rush down like waters and righteousness like a mighty stream' are Amos' words . . . This blunt speaking moral conscience of his time warns . . . as if he were speaking to us today:

"That 'the days will come, saith the Lord God, that I will send a famine in the land. Not a famine of bread, nor a thirst for water, but of hearing the word of the Lord. And they shall wander from sea to sea, and from the north even to the east. They shall run to and fro to seek the word of the Lord, and shall not find it' . . . Has anyone more accurately described the situation we face in America today? . .

"Arnold Toynbee who wrote the acclaimed 12 volume *A Study of History* once declared, 'Of the 22 civilizations that have appeared in history, 19 of them collapsed when they reached the moral state America is in today.' Toynbee died in 1975, before seeing the worst that [was as] yet to come. Yes, Arnold Toynbee saw the famine. The 'famine of hearing the words of the Lord.'

"Whether it is removing a display of the Ten Commandments from a Courthouse or the Nativity Scene from a city square. Whether it is eliminating prayer in schools or eliminating 'under God' in the Pledge of Allegiance. Whether it is making a mockery of the sacred institution of marriage between a man and a woman or, yes, telecasting around the world made-in-the-USA filth masquerading as entertainment . . . " [the prophecy is being fulfilled].

Senator Miller went on to recommend a book entitled *Original Intent*, by David Barton, and mentions one of the members of the First Continental Congress, Dr. Benjamin Rush. "When Rush was elected . . . his close friend Benjamin Franklin told him 'We need you . . . we have a great task before us, assigned to us by Providence.' Today, after 228 years or more, there is still a great task before us assigned to us by Providence. Our Founding Fathers did not shirk their duty and we can do no less.

"By the way, Benjamin Rush was once asked . . . 'are you a democrat or an aristocrat?' The good doctor answered, 'I am neither . . . I am a Christocrat. I believe He, alone, who created and redeemed man is qualified to govern him'." Pretty "scary stuff" for today's New Aristocracy on the Federal benches!

Speaking of Israel, I haven't had time to say much about the state of Israel in my columns yet, but before closing, I must mention an issue that the movie "The Passion" has brought into fashion. "Anti-Semitism." When the "scholarly" critics shout "anti-Semitism" in our packed theaters, it's a red herring, a straw-herring. What they REALLY fear is bad press for atheists and agnostics. They fear even greater solidarity of Jews and conservative Christians against the fashionable anti-Israelism now so prevalent on many of our colleges and universities.

Excerpt from *World* magazine in 2001:

"For fascists, the 'Jewish influence' is precisely that transcendence — of God, of universal moral truths, of the kinds of thought and political freedom this implies — which they hope to destroy. One difference is that Middle East fascism recognizes what Western fascists believed in private but drew back from saying in public, **that if Jews are the enemy, so are Christians."** ["The new fascists; today's terrorists have a political ideology, and we've faced it before," by Gene Edward Veith (my emphasis)]

More about that subject later, but suffice it to say that all forms of fascism — from conspiracy nuts to tenured academicians who expect their students to rotely parrot their anti-Judeo-Christian "teachings" — are essentially the kind of "elective despots" that Jefferson warned us about so clearly. As for those few conspiracy buffs that claim there's a curse on the Jews for "killing Christ," allow me to remind you that they *also* say that the Jews AREN'T REALLY "Jews" but some mountain-tribe from Asia Minor, or something **(and so they can't have it both ways)!**

In conclusion (finally): George Washington said that there is an "indissoluble union" between virtue and happiness, and through various means, despite judges and lawsuits and lawlessness, **God's Truth is still marching on (though the clock is running down quickly).**

Timing is everything

February 29, 2004

"The time is right . . . Eat leaden death, Imperialistic reactionary business administration majors." —"SDS," Vol. 1, no. 2 (Students for a Democratic Society, 1969)

THE TIME IS RIGHT? IS IT A COINCIDENCE that the Super Bowl half-time "show" and the gay "weddings" all happened just before the opening of "The Passion of the Christ"? Is it yet another "coincidence" that LaLa Land will shower awards on the films that would never win "hearts and minds" in Iraq? And they'll blacklist Mel Gibson and accuse him of insensitivity?

In the 1960s, America was in denial about a "revolution," and in the 1990s we were in denial about a Culture War. Today we are in denial that this Culture War is one with international consequences. An ordinary citizen from Wyoming said it best in a letter to CBS about the Super Bowl. Among other things, he said,

> What really bothers me is that, after reading all of the news stories, I find that CBS still doesn't realize what they did, and why it was wrong. Well CBS — here is why: American soldiers are engaged in a culture war in Iraq and Afghanistan. At this point in the battle, it's no longer our armies against their armies; it's our ideas of freedom and liberty against the enemy's ideas of fear and repression. America has put out a message of hope to the world — live

101

free, have hope, and enjoy the fruits of a free and open
. . . society. The Super Bowl half-time show poisoned
that message. Given the opportunity to share the best
of America with the world, the show's producers instead
chose to showcase the vilest, narrowest, most hedonistic
aspects of our culture — and it was broadcast to the biggest
world-wide audience CBS will have all year . . .

It's not my job to comment on the decision to go to Afghanistan
or Iraq, but once America (and Britain) decided to go, let it be
known that our English Bible translations say, "When you go to war
against your enemies, keep you from every evil way." The Iraqi
people must be wondering how we can straighten out *their* mess if
we don't even follow our own beliefs. Those who ask "What's the
big deal?" about the popular culture, sadly, wouldn't know a "big
deal" if it clobbered them upside the head.

Point is: Satan consistently gets humans to go at least one step
"too far"! The radical "Students for a Democratic Society" set
back their own socialist agenda light years by their own radical
nature. The Super Bowl "show" set back "artistic freedom" a
decade or two. In 2004, the social engineers and "pro-active"
judges had us right where they wanted us until the mayor of
San Francisco decided to promote gay "marriages" contrary to
a law specifically voted into law by California voters. Don't be
"shocked" if his decision and the spurious "weddings" backfire on
their own "cause"!

I realize that the cultural revolutionaries hate history even
more than the subject of economics, but history contains lessons
they would be wise to learn. One of those lessons is **timing is
everything!** An interesting quote from a history book:

"[Little] more than a year before the Declaration of
Independence was issued, Washington wrote to a friend in England
that the idea of separation from Great Britain was not entertained
by any considerable number of the inhabitants of the colonies.
If Independence had then been proclaimed, it would not have
been supported by public sentiment and its proclamation would
have excited hostilities and promoted divisions which might have
proved fatal to the cause. Time, — the development of events,

— the ripening of conviction of the necessity of such a measure, were indispensable as preliminary conditions of its success." — Henry J. Raymond in *The Life, Public Services and State Papers of Abraham Lincoln* (1865)

Raymond was making the point that Lincoln was wise enough not to issue the Emancipation Proclamation too early, when it would have driven the Border States into the Confederacy. This relates to issues now facing leaders from Sacramento to Boston. President Bush claims to be working on cultivating a "culture of life" with regard to human life issues, but events forced him to take an early stand on a Constitutional Amendment to define marriage as "man-and-woman" (how "radical").

Do not take these issues lightly. At Gettysburg, Lincoln said, "We are now engaged in a great Civil War, testing whether this nation or any nation so conceived and so dedicated can long endure." At the Harvard Law School Forum in 1999, Charlton Hesston said: "Those words are true again. I believe that we are again engaged in a great civil war, a cultural war that's about to hijack your birthright to think and say what resides in your heart . . . I serve as a moving target for the media who've called me everything from 'ridiculous' and 'duped' to a 'brain-injured, senile, crazy old man.'"

Andy Rooney recently called Mel Gibson "crazy." Evidently Gibson's on the "wrong list" too! For the Left, the worst thing that could have happened right now is a popular movie about, **of all people, Jesus Christ. The timing is just all "wrong"! It's Academy Awards week!**

If Rooney or anyone else thinks that "The Passion" is about Mel Gibson or "prejudice," they've missed the point! It's about you. It's about me. It's about sin - and the cost of redeeming our sorry S&H green stamps! It's also a bit about rulers in high places in this world.

One reason people take "The Passion" as ominous is because they seem to sense somehow that God is about to force some "decisions" and they fear that when He stands at the door and knocks, they'll go to the back door.

Many people believe that "ambassadors of Christ" should be opinion-less and toothless. Nothing could be further from the truth, even analogously. Our #1 ambassador, Colin Powell, said the other day that the Haitian president's "time may be about up." I recall one time when our ambassador to the Philippines had to say essentially the same thing to President Marcos. What's the real "mission" of an ambassador of Christ then?

The apostle Peter, who once betrayed Christ three times, later assigned us "ambassadors" a MISSION: "For so is the will of God, that with well doing you may put to silence the ignorance of foolish men: As free . . ."

As the "freest" nation on earth, the operative principle that applies to America is: "Unto whom much is given, much shall be *required*"! This applies to every segment of our society: young and old, left and right, rich and poor, believers AND non-believers.

In *The Religion of Abraham Lincoln* (1963), William Wolf says:

> *The Puritan heritage distilled through the 18th century patriots without, however, loss of its original religious strength explains many features in Lincoln's thought. It is the background for the predestinating will of God, for corporate and individual responsibility, for the direction of democracy as a way, for America as 'God's almost chosen people,' for belief in the wisdom of the people, for the possibility of making a solemn vow and covenant with God and observing its historical results, for the importance of 'discerning the signs of the times . . . ' His political action, as revealed by his own words, was ultimately the social expression of an understanding of God and of man that demanded responsible activity. This is contrary to a widespread modern opinion that religion should be a* **separate interest or even a hobby in life** *. . .*

That last line sums up the zeitgeist — "the spirit of our age." People in elite positions in education and the media believe that going to church is almost but not quite on a par with going to the gym, or going to the bathroom (perhaps "harmless"). But a believer is considered "unfit" to hold the office once held by the Great Emancipator [which sounds kinda "judgmental" to me]!

I don't know why but the question occurs to me, what would be my parting advice should I never write anything again? For some reason, the line that comes to mind is by Yogi Berra: **"When you come to a fork in the road, take it."**

I'm not "selling" anything. I wouldn't try to sell you my religion, nor Mel Gibson's, and if you're turned off by "organized" religion, you could always start your "own" religion. You could call it something like the Fellowship of Anyone Not Teaching Absent-minded Students to Ignore Christ (or His commandments). **FANTASTIC.** I'm being partly facetious here, but not entirely.

By the way, I don't know why "Lefties" are so upset with "white collar crimes" these days. *They're the ones who taught us that "there are no moral absolutes," "if it feels good do it," and "the only eternal verity is change"!* "White collar criminals" may have followed suit, but the moral relativists are the ones who LED that suit!

In the February 13, 1997 Hagar the Horrible strip, the sidekick Lucky Eddie says, "Hagar, explain to me again the 'Viking theory of economics.'" Hagar says:

"Well, some people have too much stuff. It's the Viking's job to relieve them of some of their stuff so it gets spread around."

Eddie says, "What if they come and take their stuff back?" and Hagar says:

"Now you're talking about STEALING!"

And many a truth was spoken in jest. Have a nice week!

No more bull

March 19, 2004

"Blessed be the name of God for ever and ever; for wisdom and might are His; He changes the times and the seasons: He removes kings and sets up kings." —Daniel

THROUGH A SERENDIPITOUS FLUKE of divine intervention, Abraham Lincoln finds himself resurrected, and instantaneously being interviewed by the "60 Minutes" program:

60 Minutes: Mr. Lincoln, the first question is, how do you feel about same-sex marriage?

Lincoln: Uh, my ears must have been damaged by the gunshot; I thought you said same-sex marriage.

60 Minutes: You heard the question, Mr. President. Do you believe in a Constitutionally guaranteed right to gay marriage?

Lincoln: Well, uh, if that's the question, I suppose Mary and I had a fairly gay marriage. She was gayer than I was though; some people said that I was WAY too serious!

60 Minutes: Answer the question, Mr. President. Should people have the right to legally marry someone of their own gender with a Constitutionally guaranteed right to a marriage license?

Lincoln: Sounds to me as if it has become nothing but a piece of paper.

60 Minutes: You mean the Constitution or a marriage license?

Lincoln: BOTH. But just for curiosity, what's the next question?

60 Minutes: The question is, do you believe that a woman has a Constitutionally guaranteed right to an abortion on demand?

Lincoln: **Don't tell me; we've fallen under the influence of the Europeans again, haven't we? That reminds me of a story . . .**

[Cut away to commercials for the National Organization for Women and Preparation-H.]

Yes, boys and girls, the magic word for the day is "bull." I just got back from vacation, and on the trip I passed through Buncombe County, NC (as in "bunkum"). My book on word origins says that there are three distinct words in English for "**bull.**" The one I want to focus on is the third one:

"ludicrous or self-contradictory statement, usually in the phrase   'Irish bull,' whose origins are mysterious; there may be a connection with the Middle English noun *bul* ('falsehood') or the 15th century verb *bull* ('mock' or 'cheat')."

So if you thought I was starting to use vulgar English, you can take a deep breath. When the Kingdom of God is established on earth, besides no more pain and no more tears, there will be no more **bull** - no more lying (with statistics or otherwise).

By the way: If the approximately one percent of the population who are working farmers began agitating for marriage licenses for cows and bulls, and bulls and bulls, they would be ignored more than laughed at, but the above "interview" of Lincoln by 60 Minutes illustrates, I hope, how badly our litigious society has become distracted and derailed. The often-accepted figure of 10% as the size of the gay population is a "ludicrous and self-contradicting statement" (see "The Shrinking Ten Percent," Time magazine, April 26, 1993):

"YOU'VE HEARD THE NUMBERS — 10% OF AMERICAN MEN ARE GAY, 2.7 million children are abused . . . Politicians, activists, fundraisers, scientists and, yes, magazine journalists routinely unload such staggering statistics on a trusting public. The numbers are presented as though they carry all the weight of scientific truth. Don't believe it . . . Statistics on crime, poverty, homelessness, joblessness, drug abuse, toxic hazards, sexual harassment . . . are notoriously suspect . . . [A recent] study, one of the most thorough reports on male sexual behavior ever, found that only 1% of the 3,321 men surveyed said they considered themselves exclusively homosexual."

Please note: That's a quote from *Time*, which has a cover story saying that it's "okay" now for mothers to stay home and take care of their children! Anyway, if the stat for gays is now anywhere near 10%, there must be a whole lot of recruitin' goin' on out there!

People claim that "you can't legislate morality," but as a comic strip once put it, "Immorality is easy" (especially if you *promote it* in the public schools)!

In his book, "The Life, Public Services and State Papers of Abraham Lincoln" (1865), Henry J. Raymond tells the story of a visit to Lincoln by a Colonel McKaye. McKaye had been to visit freed slaves in the South. He told about a group of freedmen who were discussing their concepts of power:

They had an idea of God, as the Almighty, and they had realized in their former condition the power of their masters. Up to the time of the arrival among them of the Union soldiers, they had no knowledge of any other power. Their masters fled upon the approach of our soldiers, and this gave the slaves the conception of a power greater than their masters exercised. This power they called "Massa Linkum."

Colonel McKaye said that their place of worship was called "the praise house," and the leader of the "meeting," a venerable black man, was known as "the praise man." On a certain day, considerable confusion was created by different persons attempting to tell who and what "Massa Lincoln" was. In the midst of the excitement, the white-haired leader commanded silence.

"Brederin," said he, "you don't know nosen' what you're talkin' 'bout. Now you jus listen to me. Massa Linkum, he be every whar. He know every ting."

Then, solemnly looking up, he added: *He walk de erf like de Lord.* Colonel McKaye told me that Mr. Lincoln was very much affected by this account. He did not smile, as another would have, but got up from his chair and walked in silence two or three times across the floor. As he resumed his seat, he said, "It is a momentous thing to be the instrument, under Providence, of the liberation of a race!"

The purpose for recounting the story above is to put some things in context, to show the contrast between the seriousness with which some Presidents have viewed their power and the way our present one is treated by our "high and mighty" academics and comedians, some of whom aspired to his office. Obviously, some people don't comprehend the seriousness of the condition of man, or the gravity of the world situation, especially since the bombings in Madrid, Spain.

And the media are "against violence" but have their darlings among the terrorists (for instance, the clowns who send in 10-year-old boys with bombs in their backpacks to blow up Israeli "bystanders," as if the "bystanders" had no business being there). The media call terrorists in Iraq "insurgents," as though akin to the "peace protestors" who used to march through free American streets chanting "Ho, ho, ho; Ho Chi Minh; dare to fight and dare to win."

As for the office of the President of the United States, Lincoln was neither perfect nor without critics in his own time, but Henry Raymond tells another interesting story:

"At the White House one day some gentlemen were present from the West, excited and troubled about the commissions or omissions of the Administration. The President heard them patiently, and then replied: 'Gentlemen, suppose that all the property you were worth was in gold, and you had put it in the hands of Blondin to carry across the Niagara River on a rope, would you shake the cable, or keep shouting to him . . . *lean a little more to the north — lean a little more to the south?* No, you would hold your breath as well as your tongue, and keep your hands off until he was safe over. The Government [is] carrying an immense weight. Untold treasures are in their hands. They are doing the best they can. Don't badger them.'"

I've even done some of that 'badgering' in this column (over legitimate issues), but since that "anti-crusade"-like attack in Spain, the time has come to get serious and "hold our breath." North or South, East or West, all Americans should pray for the President on that "tight rope." I sincerely believe he's doing the best he can.

I used to have a boss who would often say, "It's a great day for the race." When asked *what race*, he would smile and say, "The human race." One of the best articles I ever read was by Elliott Abrams in the May 19,1997, *National Review*: "Can Jews Survive?" The same cultural revolutions are attacking America, Britain, and the Jews. It is essentially a crisis of identity. Abrams said that "the exact opposite of what [was] expected is now happening. Jewish life that is not centered on Judaism is disappearing in America, while traditional Judaism — and above all Orthodoxy — which was expected to disappear, is stubbornly holding on."

Jewish identity both here and around the world evidently can't be preserved without the Sabbath "sign." Like runaway teenagers, it's time for Americans, Brits, and Judah to "phone home" — to get back to their *original roots*. **Otherwise, prophecy says that "evil men and seducers shall wax worse and worse" and you might as well get used to it 'til Kingdom come.**

While you pray for the President, pray for the peace of Jerusalem. "In the days of these kings shall the God of heaven set up a kingdom which shall never be destroyed." Moviemakers who now want to "cash in" on a sequel to "The Passion" might consider making one called "The Lord of the Kings; the Return of the Lamb." But don't hold your breath.

As I write this, it's the anniversary of the war against Saddam Hussein (and the last day of winter!). Some people ask, "Where are the weapons of mass destruction" — not expecting a reply. Well, this may be the dumbest question of all, but how do you know that the WMDs aren't in France, or somewhere even worse? Think about it.

Yes, it's springtime in America, and there's no time like the present for us to get back to the God who called Himself *"the God of Israel."* Daniel said that "the wise shall understand," but in the end it is ONLY the wise who will be able to experience the kind of satisfaction Abraham Lincoln felt when he said, "It is a momentous thing to be the instrument, under Providence, of the liberation of a race" [**the human race**]!

AMERICA, PLEASE PHONE HOME! NO MORE BULL!

Trials: Castor oil for the soul (or, is man nothing but pond scum?)

March 30, 2004

"Let there be light." —God

I CAN'T WAIT for the general Resurrection. I have 100,000 questions for Charles Darwin. Did the means of sexual reproduction "gradually" evolve (maybe TOO gradually?). When the first woman who had gradually developed the means of sexual reproduction met the first man who had the means of sexual reproduction, did she tell him to go lose himself in the jungle? One can see how this process could have taken billions and billions of years! Which came first, the omasum or the abomasum, etc.?

Or was it even about biology at all? Maybe it was just one woman who started yelling "Stand on your hind legs like a man, sit up straight, keep your elbows off the table, and stop dragging your knuckles on the ground!" As long as the female of the species had her head basically screwed on right, there was some hope for the future.

My parents were married 50 years. Modern humanists will have to "forgive" them, but their marriage lasted a lifetime *because of*, probably, more than *in spite of*, their trials. And, as "children of the 40s," crybabies were always told, "Quit your whining or I'll give you something to cry about." Mothers had no qualms about dangling prepositions or threats over our heads. We had heard about Hitler since we were in the womb, so that put things in perspective. Life on the farm wasn't a no-fault, no-pain situation, but parents and teachers got the job done (and we were thankful in the end).

Meanwhile, the intelligentsia had "plans" for America. The "Higher Learned" figured that since thousands of our young people had seen Paris and the rest of "Cosmotania" during WW II, the time was right for a Cultural Revolution here. Science would replace faith, and then psychoanalysis would rule the day. Very gradually, "given enough time," brainwashing by the consolidated schools and the media would eventually turn over all political power to the priests of the "New Temple" (lawyers in the Courts).

The 1800s weren't Utopia, but as Thomas Sowell says, at least the people who engaged in Wild West shootouts or lynch mobs "spared us the pretense that they were upholding the Constitution" [NewsMax magazine, Feb. 04]. But I "ramble," don't I? I'm prepared for the charge, but actually the preceding columns — like layers of a pyramid — have all been aimed toward a single **"point."** As you proceed, if you will, you can just try to figure it out **("what's the point?").**

Our "text for the day" comes from Charlie Sykes' 1992 book, "A Nation of Victims; the Decay of the American Character" (St. Martin's Press). Mr. Sykes will help you figure out where we are and how we got here. The general populace is not without culpability for allowing it all to happen, but the *instigators of our decline* hide out in tax-subsidized, ivy-covered, ivory towers.

Under the heading **The No-fault, No-pain Society,** Sykes quotes a line from "Mr. Sammler's Planet," a novel by Saul Bellow: *You wondered whether . . . the worst enemies of civilization might not prove to be its petted intellectuals who attack it at its weakest moments — attacked it in the name of reason and in the name of irrationality . . . in the name of sex, in the name of perfect and instant freedom* [quote, unquote].

Even the old Soviet slave masters had unique definitions of "freedom"; political enemies could be sent to mental hospitals, thereby "freeing" them from antiquated notions of

Traditionalism. The redefinition of "mental health," believe it or not, has even occurred in the West (through more subtle forms of "reeducation").

Writing about the late 1800s, Sykes says, "As the mainline churches fell into decline, there was an upsurge in spiritualism . . . and New Thought [essentially Utopianism] . . By the time Freudianism first arrived here, Americans were already well-disposed to listen; the groundwork had been thoroughly laid . . . Social Darwinism and the rise of an insatiable consumer society — a culture of expectations and entitlements — were the flotsam and jetsam of the triumph of science over faith and the decline of the transcendent values that had underlain the social order [including business] . . .

"The results were not what the prophets of liberation had envisioned . . . Instead of being freed from oppressive bonds of the past, [man] found himself alone in a world without mooring, norms, sense of direction, or purpose." Enter the followers of Freud, stage left:

"Filling the vacuum created by the decline of institutional faith and the collapse of the moral order it has provoked, psychoanalysis has assumed many of the functions traditionally performed by religion . . . Freud himself set the tone for the assault on faith. He regarded religion in all its forms as an illusion and therefore recast it as a form of neurosis." His disciples were "the first to insist that the church was an instance of mental disorder — of madness."

Sykes says that this New Establishment didn't need to "debate the strictures of family identity or religious faith or sexual morality when they could simply be dismissed as products of the 'authoritarian syndrome.' An unsophisticated . . . or backward-looking populace hardly needed to be argued with when it could be cured . . . *By identifying the 'liberal personality' as the antithesis of the authoritarian personality, [the intellectuals] equated mental health with an APPROVED POLITICAL POSITION*" *["The Authoritarian Personality" by T.W. Adorno, et al (1950), my emphasis]*.

This Brave New "therapeutic" society was founded on two self-contradictory premises: that human nature is basically good and can be reformed without religion, while (on the other hand) that man is, essentially, "just an animal" and has a right to *behave* like an animal if he so desires. Emotions trumped reason, and the values of the Founding Fathers were - in succession - minimized, "clarified," "debunked," and finally, tossed out altogether. So far, the plot is working like a charmed one, Satanically so!

As a farm boy, I witnessed a "trial run" of such a strategy when new methods of chemical farming were rammed down society's throat. Most of the older farmers were opposed to it, but as a practical matter, it didn't matter! The younger generations were simply "reeducated" and the geezers were allowed to die off, with our soil being the unintended victim of the mischief.

The social engineers are the most optimistic segment of today's society. They foresee nothing but victory all over again. Most of the World War II vets and their children didn't "buy" the "approved position" in the culture war, but as the producer and writer of *Ellen* once said, there are a lot of empty cemeteries out there, and when they are filled, the world will be a lot more *"tolerant"!*

The current debate between optimistic conservatives and pessimistic ones is like a "good cop/bad cop" scene in a movie. No one should be actually "hoping" for bad news, but only by being honest about the future can that future possibly be avoided — or rewritten. Optimists cite the "pendulum principle," the theory that the "pendulum" is about to swing back. They think it always does, automatically.

If there is just one point I would want to make (and I said I was going to make one), it is: THERE IS NO PENDULUM. There is no pendulum, because it may already be TOO LATE!

Personally, I'm 99 44/100 percent pessimistic, because I've been around for 60 years and have watched the cultural "line" being "pushed" and "pushed" in one direction. There's a ratchet on the "line" and it's not going to come back. And there comes a time in the history of nations when only God can save them (and also a point when even God stops listening).

The only reason I'm not 100 percent pessimistic is because I recall what happened when the intellectual elite tried to force the metric system down America's throat. We simply didn't "buy" it. But I'm afraid we've already "bought" too much of the Cultural Revolution (one definition of a hypocrite is someone who complains about all the sex on his VCR).

Supposedly, polls say that 80 or 90 percent of Americans believe in God. A more crucial question would be, "Does He believe in us?" Not if they're just "secret Christians"! Lincoln said the world would probably be better off if more "punishment" were preached, "and a little less forgiveness of sin." Thanks to Freud and social Darwinism, modernists don't even "feel" any guilt anymore. If the optimists among us saw a hand, writing on the wall, they would probably just go, "Cool!"

According to the psychology of the nanny-state, lawsuit-crazy, whiny entitlement-demanding society in which the government has replaced the father, and Mother Earth herself is the Great Mother of the Gods, the name of the game is blaming the scapegoat-of-the-day. And blaming scapegoats for every ill is just another way of saying that God is dead, or to be more exact, at least "The God of Judgment" is dead (Malachi 2:17).

As old-fashioned mothers would tell us "Quit whining or I'll give you something to cry about," I wonder what God is thinking today? "Quit your whining or — [whatever]"? One thing is obvious: our society is divided right down the middle by any measurement one could use. There comes a time in God's great stop-watch *after which* there is no holding back the hands of time. THERE IS NO PENDULUM. The modernists in the name of "progress" and "enlightenment" have dismantled Grandfather's clock and the pendulum is not going to just swing back.

If a revival *were* to occur, it could only occur the way awakenings have happened in the past: only after decades of prayer, sweat, and tears. I'm talking about prayer, sweat, and tears by individuals who are not waiting for some mass movement or mob psychology to take over — just a *PERSONAL* "thing"!

In the cartoon strip *Priscilla's Pop*, one day Priscilla asks her pastor, "When did the Christian era begin?"

He says, **"Any day now. Any day now."**

Yes, our "nation of victims" is addicted to "murmuring" (to use the King James English), like so many wanderers in the Wilderness. The habit almost seems genetic. It's time to drive the snakes out of our land, figuratively speaking.

By the way, I was once debating Darwinism on the internet with a student at a university in Sweden, and he thought he was doing great as long as the subject was biology. All of a sudden, I changed the subject to physics and asked him how light evolved. He said, "We don't say light evolved" and I said, "Yes you do; you say *everything* evolved!" But he had no answer; that means they essentially admit that the physics of light was either designed or is a supernatural phenomenon. The jig is up; the party's over.

Post-script for the Post-modern era

April 13, 2004

"Happy birthday, Thomas Jefferson." —CD

FROM THE DARK AGES to the "Enlightenment" and "Romanticism" to Existentialism and beyond, this old world keeps "recycling" itself. More than 20 wars are being waged at any one time now as we cycle through the post-Christian era toward — WHAT? — back to the future? Back to that era which followed the Age of Revelation in the first century?

Modern "thinkers" still believe that the humanist "isms" were all improvements on revelation and that most of them could have been successful if only they had been run by the "right people" (namely THEM, the modern "thinkers"). The proverbial "spectrum" runs, left to right: Communism, socialism, National socialism (fascism), "Christian" Democratic socialism, cooperativism, capitalism, and individualism. If this line were to be considered a circle in which, if one goes so far left that you become "right," they would meet at a point called "anarchy" (still to the left of Communism). No matter what angle you view the spectrum from, Fascism is still always far, far, LEFT, with Communism *more* "left."

As I like to remind people, I have on my wall at home an auto license plate from 1917 that survived in a roadside ditch longer

119

than the Evil Empire lasted. That rusty plate lasted through literally hundreds of wars and "storms of the century." And the Truth is like that license plate — buried in the sand and *forgotten* — just like the Book of the Law buried under rubbish in the Old Temple in Jerusalem.

By the way, since 20 percent of the 10 Commandments are aimed at protecting **private property,** Communism — and most of its socialist cousins that allow confiscation of private property — are out of the question (*Christian Democratic socialism* is a double oxymoron).

Our Founding Fathers such as Washington and Jefferson spoke of "truth" without blushing, and without mocking the Truth like it was mocked every week on *Laugh In* (and "that's the Truth!). Today we live in an era in which people are incapable of blushing (*at anything*) — and our children probably wouldn't know what the word "blushing" means! The last time I saw a woman blush was in 1961, and I didn't make her do it.

Anyway, we have reared a generation of "bored" teeny-boppers who flash just a little skin here and a little skin there in the name of "Freedom" and "liberty" (more exactly, "license" and *denial*). They have forgotten the history of empires because they've never been informed about all these empires that were constructed on SAND. But one can tell by their grumbling that our bored teenagers — and breathlessly sophomoric adults — are as equally disappointed by the Fruits of the Flesh as any of their forebears who took the same tack. Contemporary "fulfillment" only comes in small victories regarding even smaller issues of "victimhood."

Sometimes one has to escape to the funny papers (as we called them) to dig a little Truth out of civilization's roadside ditches. One of the most insightful comic strips is *Cathy.* In a recent strip, Cathy and her Irving are going over a "to do" list for their planned wedding. Cathy "volunteers" one by one for every item on the list (trusting no jobs to her "man"). Finally, Irving asks a dumb question: "Can someone tell me how you can be a control freak and a victim at the same time?" Cathy, of course, says **I can do that!**

The institution of marriage has been going the way of the horse and carriage in places such as Scandinavia and France, concurrent with the rise of "gay marriage." Those who would "lead" us through the Wilderness cause us to stumble by encouraging the imitation of them! With *Friends* like these, who needs enemies?

Speaking of enemies, though, although people have been anticipating WW III for decades, now that we are actually IN it, people are in complete denial. The other day, which was called "Good Friday," I was in line at the counter at the Quik Trip when I saw a man pick up a local newspaper by the other cash register. The smug, smirky look on his face instantly gave me bad vibes. I didn't hear his exact words, but the clerk came back with, "You LIKE it when people die?" Evidently, he had made a snide remark about a local boy who had just been buried, because the clerk asked him, "Have you *talked* to any of the veterans who have been *over there?*"

I was out the door, but the newspaper buyer was obviously relishing the prospects of his political buddies' return to power so that he could "cash in" on freebies in the form of "federal aid"! As the caissons go rolling along in Iraq, I recall true tales I had heard about WWII. On the day after a battle in which the Nazis had battered the Allies, a man walked into the local meat market and said to the clerk, "We really gave 'em hell yesterday, didn't we?" That clerk didn't challenge the guy, because they were both Nazi-sympathizers. Some people do "like it" when people die, and the only thing that's different now is the enemy's uniform. Now it's kids wearing backpacks or more cowardly bombers in roadside ditches.

Those who have their "eyes open" must not let the war distract them totally from the even bigger war, the war with *our selves*. We're in uncharted waters and we must not only focus on where the reefs are, but on where they are NOT. There was once a ship that became stuck in the ice. There was nothing the crew could do but sit tight and take a measurement of their position in the morning. When they did so, they found that they had actually drifted **backwards** several miles. So it goes with our personal lives sometimes.

These columns are my attempt to gauge and convey the latitude and longitude of civilization's "position," and it is an understatement to say that we are ADRIFT. Even many churches are drifting "down the river" or sometimes backwards along the muddy backwaters with the Popular Culture (PC), frozen in ice. And if treachery abounds even at your local Quik Trip, one can only imagine the international intrigue going on behind the curtain.

We exist at a time of vast international poker games and Russian roulette. They "shall speak lies at one table" and "the heathen assemble and imagine a vain thing." He who sits in the heavens shall laugh; "the Lord shall have them in derision." Their arrows shall enter into their own hearts because they imagine in vain that they can build a successful secular society on the ashes of the failed Evil Empires of the past.

My critics may say, "If you know so much, why have you spent the last 40 years climbing trees?" My answer is, because they were *there*, like the Grand Teton (that I climbed in 2002). That's an aside, but at least if they ask me *Have you been to the mountaintop?* I can say "Yes," and if they ask me *Which one?*, I can tell them.

On August 23, 1966, I stopped at a Wisconsin Welcome Center on the Interstate highway and overheard a conversation between the smiling, blonde girl behind the counter and a man and his boy. She asked the little boy, "Where are you from?" and he said, "Berwyn."

The father said, "Tell her what state you're from?" And the little boy said:

"AMERICA."

I had to get back in my car and drive away because I couldn't hold back the tears. The fall was coming and terrible times were on the horizon beyond the rolling hills. I've shed a lot of tears for our "state" and our "country" over the last 40 years. In his farewell to the United Nations, President Reagan said, "Your young men shall see visions and your old men shall dream dreams." And I've been there, both as a young man and an old.

Critics or no critics, in other eras, tree cutters were one of the most important parts of an army, because they cut the path through the forest for the rest of the army. My, how our status has fallen! I was once working on a city beautification project, cutting out some dead and crowded trees when a little boy walked up to me and said, "Why are you cutting down the forest?" I said, *"Does this look like a forest to you?"* And he said, "Yeah, sort of."

I often think about that PC little boy and the little boy "from Berwyn" (who would be in his forties now), because they are now in the Third World War, whether they know it or not. It's essentially a spiritual war, but the "suicide terrorists" aren't religious people. Whether they realize it or not, they are the same old Nazis, speaking other languages.

Abraham Lincoln told a story about a roadside bandit who stuck a gun in someone's back and said, "Stand and deliver, or I shall have to shoot you, and then you will have made me a murderer." Terrorist organizations AND modern Academia say, "Deliver us your children, and we will save civilization." But they will only "save" your children by destroying them.

Gene Edward Veith, Jr. says, "Although Postmodernists tend to reject traditional morality, they can still be very moralistic. They will defend their 'rights' to do what they want with puritanical zeal . . . They want not only license but approval. Thus tolerance becomes the cardinal virtue . . . The Postmodernist sins are 'being judgmental,' 'being narrow-minded,' 'thinking that you have the only truth,' and 'trying to enforce your values on anyone else.' Those who question the Postmodern dogma that 'there are no absolutes' are excluded from the canons of tolerance. The only wrong idea is to believe in truth; the only sin is to believe in sin." [Postmodern Times; a Christian Guide to Contemporary Thought and Culture (Crossway Books)]

Veith repeats the Psalmist's question, "When the foundations are being destroyed, what can the righteous *do?*"

Or — as Detective Colombo would say, "Just one more *question*": **"When the Lord comes, shall He find [any] faith on the earth?** Even more relevant to you personally, "If your life ended today, do you know that you would live again?" If, to answer the question, you say, "I don't know," **there's your ANSWER.**

Whatever your answer was, I want to repeat: "What can we DO?" Unlike Jonah, who was hoping that the sinners would just "get it," I'm specifically making the official request that you actually "get the point" and honestly make a decision. Modernists like to say, "Think globally; act locally." I say: **"Act individually, but think universally."**

Abraham Lincoln said, **"LET US BE NEITHER SLANDERED FROM OUR DUTY BY FALSE ACCUSATIONS AGAINST US, NOR FRIGHTENED FROM IT BY MENACES . . OF DUNGEONS TO OURSELVES. LET US HAVE FAITH THAT RIGHT MAKES MIGHT, AND IN THAT FAITH LET US, TO THE END, DARE TO DO OUR DUTY AS WE UNDERSTAND IT."**

I second the motion, and may your young men see visions and your old men dream dreams. The flip side of beating your spears into pruning hooks is "beat your plowshares into swords." I hope that you do not overlook the obvious: **we do have a choice.**

President Reagan and President Lincoln (and I) have now said our piece, so you can take it or leave it. It's up to **YOU!**

THE END

Oh -- sorry, but just one more question . . .

May 1, 2004

"Regular people helped to build this country too, you know." —Curtis (the comic strip, 4/30/04)

GIVEN THE LUXURY of being able to conclude this book whenever I so decide, I think it's time we do some summarizing. While I admit that these columns have been light on human remedies and solutions, and heavy on problems, it's because there are so many of those. Optimistic conservatives are within their rights to list their reasons, but it's going to take a lot more than "right election results" and scattered signs of growing conservatism among our collegians to "make a difference"! We just don't seem to realize how really desperate the world is for the Kingdom!

As for the problems, which we underestimate at our own peril, we've talked here about social Darwinism and Freudianism, the public school agendas and grandiose academic plots, the incestuous news and entertainment media, and the flabbiness of our mental and physical condition as a populace. Essentially, what we are contending with are the postmodern Scribes and Pharisees and their "clients" — the regular people they so look down upon (whom they at the same time so desire to "lead").

In short, if there is a theme running through this book, it is that our "petted intellectuals" contradict themselves almost every

125

time they speak or write, and as John Dewey predicted, their faddish ideas have had a "profound" effect on the understanding of philosophy, religion, and morality. "Professing themselves to be wise," Paul predicted, "they became fools, because that, while they 'knew' God, they worshipped the creation more than the Creator, and became vain in their IMAGINATION" [ala the old Beatles tune].

The problem is, essentially, ANTHROPOMORPHISM: placing man on the same plane as animals instead of created "in the image of God." As President Nixon would say, "Let me just say this about that, and be perfectly clear":

The historical figure known as Adam was NOT just a chimpanzee that started to shave his legs! At the same time, far be it from me to say that this is a 6,000-year-old "flat earth." That's just a sorry straw man set up to be easily knocked down. I've seen the effects of weather, time, and water on the peaks of the Tetons. There is no conflict between true science and true religion, only between "lesser versions" of them. Neither science nor religion has a monopoly on hogwash and bull, so let's list some of the methods that the deceivers utilize:

- Generalizations

- Abuse of coincidental "cause-and-effect conclusions"

- Appeal to peer pressure (mass psychology)

- Appeal to false "authority"

- Faulty analogies

- Disingenuous use of statistics

- Straw men and red herrings

Last but not least are the meaningless, but focus-group-tested catchphrases endlessly repeated until they have had their Hitlerian effect. Our adversaries include secular "scribes" who invoke "environmentalism" or a false version of "equality." As a

Bible student, I expected evil to be called "good," but nothing is more shocking or foreboding than the extent to which previously considered "good" ideas have been demonized by the dominant academics, both secular and ecclesiastical.

Regarding the latter, Jefferson wrote in a letter, "I have sworn upon the altar of God eternal hostility against every form of tyranny over the mind of man." On the other side of the coin, he said in another letter:

"These are the absurdities into which those run who usurp the throne of god, and dictate to him what He should have done. May they, with all their metaphysical riddles, appear before that tribunal with as clean hands and hearts as you and I shall. There, suspended in the scales of eternal justice, faith and works will shew their worth by their weight." - Adams Extracts, p. 384

Biological theory has gone so far "out there" as to become a form of religion that requires more "faith" than the True Religion, and "you shall know them by their fruits." I think Columbo would have made a great interrogator at the celebrated "Scopes" trial by asking "just a few more" of those unasked, and unanswered, questions (for further reading, I suggest www.doesgodexist.org).

There are three reasons I undertook this writing project at a fairly advanced age: message, message, message. The Word says that we are "epistles" — or "letters" — of Christ. And I honestly thought this "letter" was finished until the other day when my Bible opened, almost by itself, to the following words of Solomon:

"When your people be smitten before the enemy because they have sinned against you, and shall return and confess your name and bow to intercede before thee towards this house, then hear thou from the heavens and forgive the sin of thy people."

The question of "who killed Christ" is a moot one, since He's not dead! Lincoln called us "God's almost chosen people," but I would drop the "almost"! We have simply been TOO blessed — and too forgetful of the blessings — for us to ignore the parallels with the people of the Wilderness. Some of America's blessings have resulted, directly and indirectly, from being a haven for millions of Jews, but that alone doesn't explain the totality of the blessings.

Speaking of the Wilderness, by the way, I climbed the Grand Teton (13,770 feet) a couple of years ago (to celebrate my 60th birthday). I went out there just for the fun of it, but found that there were some larger lessons to be learned up there on the mountain.

I couldn't have made it without a guide for one thing, and approaching the final climb we were walking along a wide ledge when all of a sudden we came to what looked at first to be a "dead end." The ledge became about 6 inches wide, and you had to shuffle your feet side-to-side, as if walking on the outside of a wooden deck, with your belly against the railing — only in this case you can't see your feet, and it's a 2,000 foot drop behind you (don't look down). One picks and chooses his handholds carefully when it's your "first time," but we all made it to the next pitch without much delay.

I wish you could all make that climb while there is still time in your life. Analogously, America is still on the "easy" part of the ledge, but the larger lesson of the mountain is:

IT GETS HARDER TOWARD THE END! Situations may well get worse before they "get better"!

Mountain guides have found that kids who successfully climb the Grand have done things with their fathers. A man and his boy were hiking a mountain trail when they came to an especially high peak from which it seemed they could see 'forever'; the father asked, "How far do you think it is from the East to the West?"

"Too far to measure," said the boy. And his father said, "So great and measureless is God's love." They stood for a moment looking in all directions, as Abraham and Isaac must have. Finally, the boy said:

"Father, then we are right in the center of God's love."

Mountaintops can do that to a person. While the ocean is wide, "East to West," and provides a bit of perspective, the Word says LOOK UP! "Up" goes on forever, and there is a slogan in shooting, "Keep your sights high" (especially when weary).

There was "just one more" lesson to be learned during my Teton climb. We can't stay on the mountaintop very long, because there's work to be done in the valley, and on the descent, we took a shortcut by doing a 120-foot overhanging rappel down to a 4- or 5-foot ledge. We could not see the ledge itself. You have to take your guide's word for it that the ledge is there!

"The point was the most dangerous place . . . It was also a great confluence of life, and the combination of peril and substance sent the spirit spinning into various ethereal regions, in which a man might be tempted to commit philosophy." — Tim Cahill in *Pecked to Death by Ducks*

I couldn't have written a script for it, but a fellow climber just happened to be one of my nemeses, a university philosophy professor! Later that evening, from a local establishment looking back toward the mountain, I asked the good professor, "Did you ever, in your whole life, ever imagine yourself near the top of the Grand Teton with a conservative at the other end of your belay line?" He said with a smile:

"I thought there was a lot of slack in the line!"

Yes, boys and girls, there can be such as thing as "too much slack" when you say to your elders, "Cut me some slack"! And the final lesson I want to infer from the climb is this: America is near the "mountaintop" right now — near its zenith — after which the going gets harder. We are being tested, and the man in the White House — holding our belay line, so to speak - calls himself a "conservative"! You would nonetheless be well advised to pray for him daily, if not more often than that, and as Lincoln advised, "Don't badger him."

A little boy stood one day in the sunshine. He called his mother and said, "Mother, God is smiling on me." She died and the boy grew up and obtained a high position in government. His goal was now to win the smiles of people in power, but one day he happened to look into his mother's diary. It opened to a page in which it read:

Today when I came out into the garden, my son was standing in the sunshine and called to me, Mother, God is smiling on me!

From that day on, the man's goal was to find his mother's God again. And when he did, God's smiles of love, joy, and peace returned to his soul. [- Today With God]

We need more of that, because this "global" world is becoming a never-never land; it just keeps getting "curiouser and curiouser." There's an eery description of this post-Christian world in the Living Psalms and Proverbs:

"Born to be bad, they have turned their backs upon the Lord, and despised the Holy One of Israel. They have cut themselves off from My help."

Mr. Taylor's version here is right on "the money"! Intoxicated with prosperity and self-preoccupation, the "non-traditionalist" society has cut its lifeline, its belay line. A fall is coming. We have 24-hour instant news, but lies are carried to the four corners of the earth at the speed of light. No one talks about mass graves in Iraq, or weapons of mass destruction captured in Jordan.

The powers-that-be in academia and the dominant media imply that there is bad hatred and "good" hatred, bad prejudice and "good" prejudice, bad terrorism and "good" terrorism, but of course "no such thing as good and evil"! As a Bible student, I expected evil to be called "good," and it is, but nothing is more shocking — or foreboding — than the extent to which previously understood good ideas are now "spun" as evil or hateful ideas.

Even a rising anti-Israelism is becoming prevalent on modern colleges and universities. "Palestine" has become a "cause du jour" with the news media. For what it's worth, the Encyclopaedia Britannica, 11th edition, says:

"PALESTINE, a geographical name of rather loose application. Etymological strictness would require it to denote exclusively the narrow strip of coast-land once occupied by the Philistines, from whose name it is derived."

Christ never referred to His region as "Palestine" and the term only appears a few times in the Old Testament, always under ominous contexts, as in "Rejoice not, whole Palestina, when your enemy is smitten."

A little boy came rushing into the house and told his mother, "There's a boy out in the woods, and when I say 'Who are you?' he says, 'Who are you?'

When I say, "I'm going to punch you in the nose," he says, 'I'm going to punch you in the nose.'"

His mother laughed and said, "That's just the echo of your own voice. If you had said, 'I love you,' you would have gotten the same response." (There must be a lesson in there somewhere).

In 1812, the news of war was delivered from Washington to New Orleans by a single rider who rode for two weeks. He could barely stay in the saddle, but he delivered the message to the governor. I've been writing for over nine months without a ghost writer, but thanks to the microchip and the personal computer, I think I've made my point. It would require ANOTHER whole book to deal with the Middle East and its prophecy ramifications, but I pray that this one will suffice for the moment, and that it will be a catalyst to propel you toward much more reading in the future.

INCIDENTALLY, the last book of the Old Testament pictured the telephone, the modem, and the Internet when Malachi said, "Then those who feared the Lord spoke often one with another, and a book of remembrance was written of them."

Thanks for reading NO MORE BULL: AMERICA, PLEASE PHONE HOME. And as Red Skelton used to say, "God bless!"

Oh -- I'm very sorry, but just "one more thing . . . "

May 5, 2004

"I have *somewhat* to say unto thee." —Jesus

SOMETIMES THE "CHOIR" NEEDS SOME PREACHIN', TOO. One thing I'm sure the Almighty could say to most of us is: "What have you done for Me, *lately?*" [No offense intended for the non-Christian community.]

A minister's little boy was watching his father work on a sermon one day. The preacher finally said, "What's on your mind, son?" The little boy asked if God inspired his sermons, and the father said, "Yes!" So the boy said:

"Then why do you cross out so much of it?" Good question.

By the way, I think I outdid Columbo in my last column. After saying "Just one more question," I forgot what the question was. I started talking about the mountains and got carried away. I'd better bring this to its "grand finale" before my brain gets any older than it already is.

My book is going to contain a little something for everyone, of course — especially for those who are looking for signs of conservative "rambling" — but I have three final questions: Who are we? How did we get here? And, what is the purpose for which we were born?

Right now one our biggest problems is *inertia!* Apathetic people tend to remain motionless, while those who are pushing the "envelope" of morality and good taste tend to remain in motion and pick up speed! His interview with *Sports Illustrated* brought John Rocker almost to "disgrace," but when that magazine subsequently published a swimsuit issue with a topless model on the cover, the editor was asked to "apologize" and sent to "sensitivity classes" — NOT! The theory is, in that case, that the "Neanderthals" had better NOT be "offended" **OR ELSE!**

Gen. Douglas Mac Arthur once said that "if the problem is of the spirit, the solution must be of the spirit." I may be paraphrasing, but no amount of rephrasing of that sentence will make a dent in the young "skulls" at the local mall. The word *spirit* simply "does not compute." They are unequipped to understand such things.

I may be getting "senile," but words matter, and history matters, so I *still* like to describe the interesting tidbits of history that somehow seem to escape the people we actually **PAY** to teach our kids. One of those tidbits is the fact that James Monroe was an actual combat soldier during the War of 1812, immediately prior to becoming the next President! So? So I submit that he is far, far more qualified than most of us to have said what he said:

*"Had the people . . been less intelligent, less independent, less virtuous, can it be believed that we should have been blessed with the same success? While then [America] retains its sound and healthful state, everything will be safe . . . It is only when the people become ignorant and corrupt, when they degenerate into a populace, that they are **incapable of exercising the sovereignty.**" — First Inaugural Address*

Does that not prove my point? How many kids at the mall today would be able to read that and make heads or tails out of it? I once saw a girl writing a nasty note to someone, and she asked me, "How do you spell *dummy?*" As general rule, we have become ignorant, corrupt, AND apathetic.

Here's another historical tidbit: when John Kerry attended that demonstration in April of 1971 where he threw his "medals" away, the man who made it possible for him to attend that day was President Nixon, upon the advice of Pat Buchanan (just one of those paradoxes that make history such a fascinating subject). The Chief Justice of the Supreme Court had granted authorities permission to remove the protestors from the Mall, but Nixon had allowed them to stay.

Nixon is a 4-letter word to some people, but I want to quote something he wrote back in 1962 when he was nothing but a former Vice-President, a failed Presidential candidate, and an unsuccessful candidate for governor:

"'[Are we] a deeply religious people[?]' To be sure, Americans are churchgoers . . They pledge allegiance to the flag of 'one nation under God' [except now in the Ninth Circuit] while the coin of the realm states . . that their trust is in God . . But what do we have here? Evidence of a basic faith that is widely shared and deeply felt, **or simply outward signs of public piety, a verbal hangover from an era long since gone? . . They are the outward form rather than the inner substance of a people's faith.**

"The strength of a nation's faith in God can be measured only in terms of the personal faith of each of its INDIVIDUAL CITIZENS. So for our own country, only to the extent that individuals have made personal commitment to that faith can America be truly characterized as a nation strong in its devotion to God . . .

"During the years that I spent in Washington, I had the privilege of hearing some of the greatest religious leaders of our generation . . But if I might dare to venture a comment, I think that some of our voices in the pulpit today tend to speak too much about religion in the abstract, rather than in the personal, simple terms which I heard in my earlier years. More preaching **from** the Bible, rather than just **about** the Bible, is what America needs . .

"The American people will not fail if they are summoned to their ultimate commitments and duties, and are recalled to the faith of their fathers. Way down inside they know that **the fads and fancies and false values of the passing scene count for** nothing . . In the face of the challenge, I for one shall look with fresh interest in the days ahead to learning what the Bible has to say to our time." —*Decision* magazine, November 1962 (just following the Cuban Missle Crisis), my emphasis.

The later Nixon, of course, made "mistakes," and other Presidents since have made "mistakes" (often without resignation or an inkling of regret). New research says that man is "hard-wired" to seek God, but if one works at it hard enough, and long enough, this wiring can be overcome and by-passed. Sin can in some cases almost be savored and *relished* at the same time it is being called a **"mistake."**

That reminds me of a story ("ramble, ramble"). A popular, but vice-prone public figure goes to his clergyman for "counsel." "I wish to confess the sin of vanity," he said. "Every time I look in the mirror, I think how handsome I am."

The pastor looks at him for a while and says, **"That's not a sin; that's a MISTAKE!"**

Would that I could be so blunt as a writer. The habit of calling a sin a *"mistake"* is to *palliate* the conscience, so that's one of the words for the day. Webster says that to "palliate" means, 1, to cloak, to lessen the pain or severity of without *curing* it; 2, to make a crime (etc.) appear less serious than it is, to excuse, to gloss over."

A palliative is related to the word *pall as in pallbearer*. The verb "pall" means "to make vapid or insipid, to render spiritless." If you stop and think about it (no speed-reading allowed here for the moment), maybe this adds some meat to Mac Arthur's concise little gem, "If the problem is of the spirit, the solution must be of the spirit."

Pat Swindall, the former Congressman, raised a cogent point in his book "A House Divided." He cited Coca-Cola's decision to scrap its original formula and replace it with a "New Coke." That went over like a proverbial lead balloon, but unlike the public schools, the company didn't stubbornly cling to its "mistake." Those in charge were not so bull-headed as to "palliate" their decision, but quickly "turned back the clock" and restored "Classic Coke." That turned out to be a brilliant decision, because a lot of people such as myself had begun to crave the "Old Coke" during its absence — even if we hadn't usually been Coke drinkers.

There's a lesson in there. The absence of God in the public schools has caused many people to crave a return to times more typical of our nation's first 200 years. However, it will take a lot more than election victories and reverse social engineering. We were warned back in the 1700s and 1800s that the road to democratic despotism is a one-way street. As President Kennedy said of the Soviets, "What's theirs is 'theirs,' and what's ours is 'negotiable.'" So it goes with modern liberalism, and here is what Alexis de Tocqueville had to say about "elective despotism":

"I seek to trace the novel features under which despotism may appear in the world. The first thing that strikes the observation is an innumerable multitude of men all equal and alike, incessantly endeavoring to procure the petty and paltry pleasures with which they glut their lives . . . Above this race of men stands an immense and tutelary power, which takes upon itself alone to secure their gratifications, and to watch over their fate . . . It would be like the authority of a parent, if, like that authority, its object was to prepare men for manhood; but it seeks on the contrary to keep them in perpetual childhood: it is well content that the people should rejoice, provided they think of nothing but rejoicing . .

[Such a government] chooses to be the sole agent and only arbiter of that happiness: it provides for their security . . . regulates the descent of property, and subdivides their inheritances — what remains, but to spare them all the care of thinking and all the trouble of living . . .

It covers the surface of society with a network of small complicated rules, minute and uniform, through which the most original minds and the most energetic characters cannot penetrate, to rise above the crowd . . . till each nation is reduced to nothing better than a flock of timid and industrious animals, of which government is the shepherd . . . Every man allows himself to be put in leading-strings, because he sees that it is not a person or a class of person, but the people at large that holds the end of his chain." —*On Democracy, Revolution, and Society: Selected Writings*, Univ. of Chicago Press, 1980, ed. by John Stone and Stephen Mennel, quoted in *Christianity and the Constitution by John Eidsmoe*

What a PROPHETIC statement! Our society is morphing into a combination of the worst aspects of both *1984* and *Brave New World* (with the 2-way computer "eye" of Big Brother, plus nearly mandatory casual sexual encounters), and obviously the **"tutelary power"** is modern academia and the dominant media, and the "Nanny State." They label anyone who questions their authority "flat-earthers" or "cultists," and the masses are told to keep repeating, "Two plus two equals five."

The magic word for the day, boys and girls, is *"conservative."* Some of my best friends cringe when I use THAT word. They want to remain apolitically "above it all," even though, were they to understand the word in the sense that I use it, they'd probably have to admit that they're "conservative" (since God never *changes*).

My trusty 38 Funk & Wagnalls defines conservatism as a principle, a "principle that is conservative, as in criticism, theology, etc." It defines "conservative" as adhering to *discipline* against novelty or alteration; not extreme; [even] *moderate* (though due to modern semantics, "moderate" has come to mean something about 180 degrees off from *conservative)!*

John Ayto says that "conserve" comes from the Latin *servare ("preserve"),* and Latin words derived from it include "praeservare" ("to guard in advance"). Given the instinct to "guard," or "watch for unintended consequences," it's no wonder that conservatives are perceived as a bit paranoid about as-yet-unforeseen events, but that's okay. Being called such names can be a badge of honor.

As for the word *cult,* I didn't know I was going there when I sat down to write, but far be it from me to "cross it out." Ayto's *Dictionary of Word Origins* says that originally the root of the word *cult* meant to "move around, turn" and it came to mean

"be busy, inhabiting a place, or making a wild place suitable for crops" [i.e., "turning" the soil].

Those meanings were channeled into Latin *"colere,"* which means "to cultivate" and also, "to worship" **and get this:** another word in the same family of words is "colony."

TRANSLATION: Farmers are "cultists" and the 13 original Colonies were in essence **13 "cults"**! Bottom line: it behooves us to "be busy" and be worshipful in cultivating both the soil and our minds, because America has reverted to being a "wild place" all over again. Remember, too, that the term "Christian" was first used as an epithet by those who hated His religion. The connotation was *cult*!

Just for the record, I wasn't in the military, but if I had to choose, I'd rather be in Baghdad than to be a policeman in our nation's Capital (maybe that's why we never draft policemen). I'd rather be in Baghdad than to be an unborn baby in the womb of a liberal woman. I'd rather be in Baghdad than be a fly on the wall in the Carville household.

Disclaimer: I didn't say we should be worshipful of the soil itself, as in "lunar soil" or "Martian soil," or "Mother Earth." I've saved a lot of trees in my life, but only in private business. I invested a lot of "sweat equity" in those trees, but no lobbying.

Way back in the 70s I received a letter from the editor of the journal for such a lobby group, and he openly admitted to me, "Most ecologists are socialists" (socialist and *pagan,* I might add). The Encyclopaedia Britannica, 11th edition says:

"GREAT MOTHER OF THE GODS, the ancient Oriental-Greek-Roman deity commonly known as Cybele . . She was also known under many other names, some of which were derived from famous places of worship . . . while others were reflections of her character as a great nature goddess: e.g. Mountain Mother . . Mother of all Gods and all Men . . In her less Asiatic aspect . . she was sometimes identified with Gaia and Demeter . . She was known as the All-begetter, the All-nourisher, the Mother of the Blest. **She was the great, fruitful, kindly earth itself."**

I could go on and on about this topic, because the priests and priestesses of these religions had a special affection for "wild nature" (as opposed to mankind). The *Britannica* cites research by Grant Showerman (Bulletin of the University of Wisconsin, No. 43, 1901) — but suffice it to say that much of what passes for Politically Correct "ecology" is in fact a New Age remnant of ancient pagan religions. It is not surprising, to me at least, that one of the "four horses of the Apocalypse" is a **green one.** The inspired Greek word in Revelation for "pale" horse comes from the root word for "chlorophyll" (i.e., green!).

One of the operative Biblical words to describe the latter-day zeitgeist is *fierce*. Politics is anything but a "game," but to many it is treated like a "game" (indeed, a vicious and a "fierce" game). I hope that our politicians do not start resorting to bench-clearing brawls such as were seen in last fall's baseball playoffs. I didn't have time to watch them, but I've seen "replays" of the one involving the shoving match between Don Zimmer and a young ballplayer. The old man ended up on the ground, and if I live a zillion years, I don't think I will ever forget that image. No matter who "started" what, our elders are supposed to get more respect than that, regardless of gender, I might add.

Divided as we are culturally, our society is almost like two people in a horse costume with two heads, one end striving for the feminization of our nation, with the other end heading off into extreme sports and unlimited "fierce" competition. If I could teach one of those "loony college courses" they now offer, I'd like to teach "competition." Competition is a word like *weather* — it can be either good or bad — so I would include the inherent positive aspects of competition, without ignoring the potential negative aspects, and I would show the video clips of the Don Zimmer brawl, because that just about says it all! "Won't it be wonderful when Iraq is just like America?"

As for those people in high places who want to drive religion underground through extreme, unconstitutional separation of church and state, I could say, "Fine, then I'll just stop praying for you," but I won't do that. I will, however, remind you that sometimes God refuses to "hear" any longer (Isaiah 1:5). If that isn't the climax you were hoping for, you can always go back and reread some of my preceding "final chapters" — or write your OWN conclusion!

I sincerely wish I could be more optimistic about the future in the short run, but we've already covered all those bases. Now if we could only figure out how to make a HOME run! Perhaps we could consult Mary and James (Matilin and Carville).

Oh, excuse me, but just one other thing! The eternally optimistic Rush Limbaugh, who believes that the stupidity in this fair land will come to a screeching halt one day, just now admitted that the stupidity just keeps on rolling. The University of Iowa cancelled a baseball game with Bradley, because the latter's nickname is the "Braves."

I almost brought up that topic when I was citing the Coca-Cola story, because I was reminded that Coke helped to steal my beloved Braves from Milwaukee. If I ever write another book, just to give you a taste of it, it might be entitled *The Year the Braves Went Back to Boston*. It would be an attempt to paint a picture of the kind of changes God wants to make on planet Earth, if it remains "alive and well."

Anyway, since pruning-hooks and plows will be so plentiful, I want to give the pruning-hooks to all the "starving artists" out there so they can go and "sculpt" some trees. The plows we'll give to the PhDs (post-hole diggers).

But the first thing I'm going to do when I get this book off my hands is to finally learn how to fish. **Because there is no free lunch, you know.** Neither is there any "free" breakfast or free supper or anything else for "starving writers." But as Christ said to His disciples, and I paraphrase, "The worst day with God is better than the best day fishing."

Thanks for reading, and if you will, pass these words on to a friend.

The End (this time I'm serious)

Epilogue: We had such HIGH HOPES, but . . .

May 7, 2004

"I have a dream." — Dr. Martin Luther King, Jr.

OUR FOUNDING FATHERS HAD A DREAM, TOO. But how much "life" is left in their dream? The acronym for "I have a dream" is **IHAD.** "It's time to get serious," as we used to say in baseball (when down 13-to-nothing!):

The most passionate "debates" these days are not between political candidates, but among those sitting on the benches of our highest courts. They refuse to "accept" the most "controversial issues," and even our theologians refuse to touch them with a 10-foot pole (citing tax exemption laws that — supposedly — separate "church" and "politics"). What these timid shepherds *really* fear is offending a few of their members sitting in the pews, while the "Silent Majority" bites the tongue, not so much out of agreement, but more out of fear of radical lawyers, bad publicity, or maybe even their mates.

Our Founding Fathers did not exhibit such gutlessness. John Adams, the one who said that our Constitution was written for a "religious" people (and inadequate for the governing of any other), often spoke of Adam, Noah, Moses, and Elijah, and of courage or virtue he wrote:

"Our dear Americans perhaps have as much of it as any nation now existing . . . But I have seen such selfishness and littleness in New England, although we are engaged in the best cause that ever employed the human heart, yet the prospect for success is doubtful not for want of power or wisdom but of **virtue."**

As for the Johnny-come-lately notion of banning God from public mention, and barring ministers from touching "controversies," Adams, et al would only laugh at that (something like this):

"[I]f a clergyman preaches Christianity, and tells magistrates [judges] that they were not distinguished from their [fellow citizens] for their private [benefit or advantage], but for the good of the people . . Oh sedition! treason!

"The clergy of this province are a virtuous, sensible, and learned set of men [usually], and they do not take their sermons from the newspapers, but from the Bible . . It is the duty of clergymen to accomodate their discourse to the times, to preach against such sins as are most prevalent, and recommend such virtues as are most [lacking] . . If public spirit is much wanted, should they not inculcuate this great virtue? . . .

"If the rights and duties of Christian magistrates and subjects are disputed, should they not explain them, show their nature, ends, limitations, and restrictions, how much soever it may *move the gall of Massachuttensis?*" — *Novanglus: A History of the Dispute with America, from 1754 to the Present*, 1774, quoted in *"In God We Trust" by Norman Cousins, 1958*

Not to change the subject but, "Believe it or Not," on the state Supreme Court building in Sacramento are engraved these words: **Send me men to match my mountains.** Some Californians today either have a strange opinion of their mountains, or manhood, but such a man was Governor Reagan, and the men God sent to our 13 Colonies.

Take Patrick Henry, whose life work not only produced *Give me liberty, or give me death*, but about one-fourth of the words at the Constitutional Convention, speaking for the minority (87-79) in favor of a Bill of Rights, and less power in the central government. Washington later asked him to be the first Chief Justice of the Supreme Court or Secretary of State, but he chose to serve five terms as Virginia's governor.

Silas Deane of Connecticut compared Henry to Demosthenes and Cicero (*God grant [that he] may not, like them, plead in vain for the liberties of their country!*). *[Eidsmoe]*

Henry's greatest contribution was pure foresight, the ability to perceive the signs of the times. John Adams said that in 1774, no other man seemed to be so aware of *the precipice, or rather, the pinnacle, on which he stood. [ibid]*

He stood in a church, by the way, for his 1775 *Give me liberty* speech, at the official Second Virginia Convention! Oh would that we had more men such as that instead of trembling before the Freedom From Religion crowd. Regarding the Stamp Act, Henry said:

This brought on the war which finally separated the two countries and gave independence to ours. Whether this will prove a blessing or a curse, will depend upon the use our people make of the blessings which a gracious God hath bestowed on us. If they are wise, they will be great and happy. If they are of a contrary character, they will be miserable.

Teachers who fail to quote the Founding Fathers are like preachers who stop quoting God, and in fact quote the *contrary!* I saw a 10 year-old boy at the library the other day who was talking about holidays, but he couldn't begin to explain the meaning of the fourth of July to his dad. So much for universal public education!

If we don't imbue kids with some *self-evident Truths* before they reach their teen years, you might as well forget it. One day at the library, I overheard two teen-aged girls at this very computer, and while checking e-mail, they were rattling off gossip at the same time: *I did him under the bleachers, and so-and-so did him under the bleachers, too and* [etc, etc.].

The superintendent of one high school claims that education is relationships! That is part of the problem, sir - too many relationships and not the slightest comprehension of Independence Day, or the difference between *liberty* and hedonistic *license!*

Eidsmoe says, "Adams' Puritan ancestors had insisted that they were engaged in an effort to establish a new and purified religious community founded on the teachings of the Bible and . . Adams, in a similar spirit, insisted that they were concerned with establishing a new and purified kind of political community, founded on the Christian religion and the precepts of John Locke [etc.]." And *speaking of "magistrates,"* a study of the first Chief Justice of the Supreme Court is WAY overdue.

John Jay was the youngest delegate to the Continental Congress in 1774, at age 29, and he and Madison and Hamilton later wrote the *Federalist Papers* (without which the Constitution might not have been ratified). Jay was a negotiator for peace treaties, and in his address to the New York Convention in 1776, aimed at securing ratification of the Declaration of Independence, his words were filled with references to Nebuchadnezzar, Jacob, Esau, and the like. He made comparisons between America and Israel, and made the point that God would not bless America's cause unless it was true to Him:

"Even the Jews, those favourites of Heaven, met with frowns, when they forgot the smiles of their benevolent Creator . . . You were born equally free with the Jews . . "

If there is chapter-and-verse for the title of this book, it is Genesis 16:8-9. The angel of the Lord came unto Hagar, Sarai's maid, and the angel said, "Where did you come from? and **where will you go?**"

Thus the title, NO MORE BULL: AMERICA, PLEASE PHONE HOME. We are like runaway teenagers at a water fountain "in the wilderness," and this is a critical concept to grasp, because current events also involve the offspring of Judah, Esau, and Ishmael (the Middle East and North Africa in general).

The gist of the story is that the angel told Hagar, "Return to thy mistress, and submit yourself under her hands, and I will multiply thy seed exceedingly, that it shall be counted for multitude. Thou shalt bear a son, and his hand shall be against every man and every man's hand against him, and he shall dwell in the presence of all his **brethren.**" Most Arabs know they are sons of Abraham, but I wonder if they know the rest of the story — that Hagar obeyed, and thus they existed!

And speaking of history, "Where did you come from?" is a question that matters, no matter whom you are, but the only "history" the lackeys of the left can remember is Washington's warning about "foreign entanglements." They conveniently forget the rest of his Farewell Address, especially, "The propitious smiles of Heaven can never be expected on a nation that disregards the eternal rules of order and right which Heaven itself has ordained."

Is that interesting 'literature,' but "ancient history"? There are no eternal rules of order and right in the privileged world of modern jurists. The revisionists of history can only poke holes in the armor of the "Dead White Anglo-Saxon Proponents of Sanity" while, in the post-911 universe, evil men wax worse and worse before their very eyes, on video! The sons of Hagar are beginning to decapitate Americans in Iraq. In the international games of poker and roulette, we are approaching the "end game"!

[The 5/12/04 *Detroit Free Press* carried the beheading story in its main headline, but, while the Iraqi P.O.W. abuse story was printed on page 1, the Nick Berg story was on page 6A, just above an advertisement for "Sex FOR LIFE" (TM) by a Boston clinic. How crass can we get? As they were sawing off his head, I'm sure that "lasting longer" was NOT one of Mr. Berg's desires! And all the medication in the world isn't going to cure a "sick" world!]

The consequences of thumbing our noses at George Washington's warning about "eternal rules" are both international and domestic. Jeremiah said, "Our inheritance has been turned over to strangers [including the tax collector] and our homes to aliens [self-explanatory]; we have become orphans, fatherless; our mothers are like widows; we pay for the water we drink."

That's from the Revised Standard Version (Lamentations 5) and, by the way, when purchased by the pint, a gallon of good bottled water now costs more than a gallon of gas!

Many assume that the words of Jeremiah, Ezekiel, and Isaiah do NOT pertain to us in the "21st century," but you know what the first word in *assume* is, don't you? Bad assumption, because Isaiah says, "Note it in a book, that it may be for the latter days [and the time to come *forever*], that this is a rebellious people, lying children, children who will not [even] *hear* the law the of the Lord."

People today can't even stand the sight of a granite stone bearing the words! In some of our towns and cities, people are filing lawsuits over **church bells** that are supposedly "too loud"!

The Stevenson High School in Sterling Heights, MI asked some students to pass on a few words for the yearbook in 2001. The valedictorian submitted these: "'For I know the plans I have for you,' declares the Lord, 'plans to prosper you and not to harm you, plans to give you hope and a future.'" The words were "cut" from the book because they came from the Bible, but it was announced in the paper today that she has won sort of an "asterisk," as the school agrees to place a sticker with Jeremiah's "controversial" sentence in copies of the yearbook on file at the school.

Even more "shocking" than the scripture is the fact that the ACLU helped her to make the point! I still don't believe in "the pendulum," but could this be a **sea change** at the ACLU?

But really - how low must one's "self-esteem" have to sink for someone to make a federal case out of "Hope" or Big Macs, HoHos or Ding Dongs, hot coffee or church bells? In a similar spirit, one woman put a birth-control jelly on her toast, and then sued her pharmacist for $500,000 when she got pregnant.

But what about "American racism," and "reparations" for slavery? Is there any substance to that issue? If he were with us, Dr. King would probably laugh at that one, too. If you think I'm "crazy," you probably haven't read his "dream speech" word-for-word. Actually, our erudite social "scientists" just cite slavery as a good *excuse* to shake the Founding Fathers off their "shoulders." Aside from the fact that people of color were more religious, and their families more intact and "functional" in the Olden Days, the Founders were not oblivious to slavery.

That was the main point of Lincoln's Cooper Institute speech. You want to see a "campaign speech"? I'll show you a *campaign speech!* It runs 15 pages long in a single-spaced, fine print book. If you never find the time to read it, I'll just point out a couple of facts, such as, Washington outlawed slavery in the Northwest Territories, and although the mechanization of agriculture was in its infancy, the Founders did everything they *could* to ease us out of slavery in an "orderly and right" fashion.

Speaking of **"prophecies,"** the much-maligned Jefferson was talking about slavery when he said, "Indeed I tremble for my country when I reflect that God is just, that his justice cannot sleep forever: that considering numbers, nature and natural means only, a revolution of the wheel of fortune, and exchanging of situation [between slaves and masters], is among possible events: that it may become *probable* by supernatural interference! The Almighty has no attribute which can take sides in such a contest."

Two ironies here: one irony is that this prophecy of Civil War is from *Notes on the State of Virginia* (Lee's state); the other is that Jefferson to this day is called a "Deist" (when deism definitely did NOT believe in "supernatural interference" in this world). That's not the only instance in which Jefferson used such language, either! In his first Inaugural, he said, "I join in addressing Him **whose Kingdom rules over all,** to direct the administration of affairs to their own greatest good." And as he wrote to Adams in 1823:

"It is impossible, I say, for the human mind not to believe that there is, in all this [creation], design, cause and effect, up to an ultimate cause, a fabricator of all things from matter and motion [which Einstein called *mass and energy*], their preserver and regulator while permitted to exist in their present forms, and their regenerator into new and other forms.

"We see, too, evident proofs of the necessity of a **superintending power** to maintain the Universe in its course and order. Stars, well known, have disappeared, new ones have come into view, comets, in their incalculable courses, may run foul of suns and planets and require renovation under other [supernatural] laws . . .

"So irresistable are these evidences of an intelligent and powerful Agent, that, of the infinite numbers of men who have existed thro' all time, they have believed, in the proportion of a million at least to [one], in the hypothesis of an eternal pre-existence of a creator, rather than in that of self-existent Universe." Read that again, more slowly this time.

The Founding Fathers weren't just anti-King George; they believed that only "King Jesus" could "rule over all." Today, two words in the national pledge, "under God," serve as an excuse for another lawsuit, as does the mockery that is "gay marriage." I was going to ignore the gay "one percent" from now on, but as Cal Thomas said (*World*, 1/10/04), if Christians don't stand up NOW for their beliefs, they won't have "much left to stand on" when the next issue comes along (and the "gators" — the litigators — will always try to fabricate new victim issues).

For those who still like to re-fight the Civil War (and other wars), unlike Hagar (who returned to her Mistress), the Confederates refused, resulting in the deaths of some half-million people. If that many could die in the days of the powder rifle (and the "Dahlgren gun"), how many could die in the days of the "suitcase nuke" before we wake up?

Ladies and gentlemen, boys and girls, it's time for the Great Awakening of the ten "sleeping virgins," time to fill our lamps with "oil"! It has been said that a "religious awakening" is what happens when the preacher ends his sermon, so it's time for me to put an end to all this writing (I haven't had time to ride my horse in two years, either).

And that reminds me of one final thing: of all the curses of modern life, perhaps the greatest one is urbanization. Just as Lot and his wife had to be taken by the hands to get them out of Sodom — and even as Lot, when told to "escape to the mountains," insisted on settling in a city ("just a little one") — so too our "moderns" not only "tolerate" the city but "love" it. The consequent loss of "horse sense," which $10,000 per pupil per year can never replace, could be fatal.

Farm boys *may* have smoked on occasion, but they smoked *behind* the barn, never IN the barn. Today's "kids" play with matches anywhere, and have burned down more than one apartment building. That's just one example; our "Mature audiences" of TV and movies play with fire in their very own souls, much to the dismay of their "better angels," by viewing *virtually anything* without any so-called "viewer discretion." Meanwhile, they harp and carp at us about cholesterol, pollution, and "carbs"!

I saw Jerry Reed sing a song that goes, "Yo still gonna die." It's a hilarious satire on "health nuts" and vegetarians, etc., and in the final analysis, it's true. **The point is this:** people not only worry too much, but they worry about the wrong things most of the time. **It's what comes out of our mouths (and courts) that can kill us.**

Modern Sodoma worries way too much about staying young while trying to find ways of getting rid of the old people (whether by assisted suicide, euthanasia, or incarceration in "homes"). The *USA Today* the other day had a front-page story about the finis of a TV show. A professor of "American studies" says that Friends made us aware that the 20s are the "prime of life" — and that **"youth rules."**

In the first place, if "youth rules," that's not a "good thing," (Isaiah 3) and I have made a discovery lately: the prime of life is the decade of the sixties. The good professor doesn't even have it half right, but there is a new book out with a much better analysis of "youth": *Hard America, Soft America*, by Michael Barone.

The author says that people today spend their lives from grade 1 to grade 12 in "soft America," where social promotion and coddling produce the most incompetent 18-year-olds we've ever seen. However, they spend their lives between age 19 and 30 in "hard America" where competition and reality produces some of the most competent 30-somethings ever.

Another form of coddling is practiced by the men of the cloth who preach the "smooth things" ("chicken soup" sermons), so I have "just one more question for the choir": Have you been deceived, and/or do you deceive others? There are gospels and then there are "gospels." Someone once said that "Opinions are like grandchildren; your *own are wonderful!*"

Human nature literally stinks, that is to say, people believe what they WANT to believe, oftentimes the Big Lie. We had a barn cat who went blind, and one day I saw one of our work horses urinating in the gutter. The cat heard this, and thought someone was pouring milk for her. It only took a quick taste to change her mind. Humans are slower to catch on; they seek *pablum, but don't realize they are partaking of poison at times.* God's thoughts are not our thoughts, and "If they speak not according to the law and the scriptures, there is no light in them." So open your eyes.

But I don't want to leave a bad taste in your mouth. In the famous words of Bret Favre, "We'd better start believing in something."

FINAL ANSWER: It's not so important to be serious as to be serious about the *important things.* I don't know who said that, but it's the *spiritual* things, the *long-range* things, and the *things above* that are "important." **Think on these things.**

P.S. "LOOK UP"

The shining city upon the hill,
A peculiar nation of law,
Even "as Israel of old":
New "Salem," milk and honey.

May God mend thine every ill,
And heal thine every flaw.
He shed His grace on America bold;
May God thy "gold" refine (not just the money).

He soundeth forth the trumpet, will!
It's time to stand in shock and awe.
Look up upon the mountain cold,
America the shining, America the sunny!

Look up, America, and please, **no more bull!**

It took me nine months to write this (the same time required for the birth of a baby), so don't abort this message, message, message:

- Be strong and have hope.
- Be of good courage.
- Resist your enemy — within you and without — and he will *flee* from you.

[Happy mother's Day, and as Jimmie Durante used to say, "Good night, Mrs. Calabash, wherever you are."]

ADDENDUM: Into the sunset

The last words in my manuscript were, "Goodnight, Mrs. Calabash, wherever you are." At the time I chose those words, I wasn't even sure of a specific reason, but as events have unfolded, it turns out, I guess, that that was my translation of the Gipper saying, "WELL – seeya later, Nancy."

One of the highlights of my life was the opportunity to see Ronald Reagan in person, giving a speech in 1980. Many people say that he was the greatest President since FDR or Teddy, but I would go even further, further back in time. President Reagan was one of those rare leaders who are not only a blessing to their own people, but to many nations. He was a blessing to people from Central America to Germany to Siberia, so I would compare him to Joseph, the son of Jacob (Israel), and if you know what I mean, I suggest checking out 2 Thessalonians 2:7 for a reference to the great "restrainers" of history (Daniel 11 also refers to such leaders at "the time of the end" who buy time for civilization as well as their own people).

At any rate, I hope you will reread some of the quotations from President Reagan in this book. I left out one of the most important ones though. He once said that future generations might have to ask OUR generation why **"those who had the most to lose did the least to preserve it."**

Preserving America and an accurate historical record of its roots is a mission whose success or failure is not optional. **We must succeed** if we are to honor the lives of all the forebears who went before us. Teddy Roosevelt said that shame and disgrace would be ours *"if we trail in the dust the golden hopes of man."*

Seeya later, Ronnie!

About The Author

The author is a columnist for www.RenewAmerica.us. He is semi-retired and divides his time between Wisconsin, Wyoming, North Carolina, and the Upper Peninsula of Michigan. He not only has broad horizons, but wide academic interests. His favorite is history, because his own roots go a long way back. His parents were both born before the Wrights got off the ground, and his dad saw Teddy Roosevelt speak in person. The author attended a one-room country school and won two college scholarships. He is listed as an alumnus of the University of Wisconsin-Madison (along with U.W. dropouts such as John Muir, Charles Lindbergh, and Frank Lloyd Wright - country boys all), but he also attended a private liberal arts college for a year.

The author can relate to the words of Ferrar Fenton: "I was in '53 a young student in course of education for an entirely literary career, but with a wider basis of study than is usual...Indeed, I hold my [business] experience to have been my most important field of education...Had I, on the other hand, lived the life of a Collegiate Professor, shut up in the narrow walls of a library, I . . should have had my knowledge of mankind so confined to glancing through a 'peep-hole' as to make me totally unfit for [my life's work]." – the introduction to *The Fenton Bible*

As an avid outdoorsman, he chose an outdoor career. Employees of his occupation used to be called tree surgeons, then "urban phytonarians," and finally, "arborists." Climbing has been a major part of his life ever since climbing farm silos at age 5 or 6, and to celebrate his 60th birthday, he climbed the Grand Teton in Wyoming, from which he snapped the photo on the cover.